LIFE'S INCREDIBLE:

10 KEY STEPS

Beth Robbins

KENDALL/HUNT PUBLISHING COMPANY
4050 Westmark Drive   Dubuque, Iowa 52002

Dedication

This book is dedicated to my parents who always loved and encouraged me; my husband who believed in and supported me; my children and grandchildren who are my greatest blessings; and my friends who helped this book become a reality. But, most importantly, this book is dedicated to my God for without Him I would not have the above blessings.

Contents

Preface

A lot of thought went into this book. The original idea was conceived several years ago following my initial involvement with some very successful people. Like many of you, at that time it seemed true success had fairly eluded me. It was through these associations and my willingness to listen to what they had to say, that I soon began to realize that I too could have the "good life."

I had often heard that we become who we are because of two things; the books we read and the people we associate with. After years of association, listening, reading and learning, I knew beyond a doubt, this was true. I had become more in that short time than in all the years before in terms of success—both personally and financially. What I have done is to take my experiences and through a series of short stories, quotes and pictures made what I learned available to everyone who has ever dreamed of having a better life. Within these pages lie the secrets of successful people everywhere.

Life's Incredible: 10 Key Steps is a simple, easy-to-follow series of thought-provoking short stories, quotes, poems and pictures. As you read the book, you too will become aware of the incredible potential lying within you. You'll find yourself dreaming again, planning and working toward your dreamed success—whatever it might be. An incredible life *is* waiting for you, so let's get started!

Develop a Winning Attitude I

Winners expect to win in advance.
Life is a self-fulfilling prophecy.

Attitude is the single most important character trait in achieving the things in life you have always dreamed of having and therefore the first step of your journey toward an incredible life. A poem by Charles Swindoll titled *Attitude* hangs on my office wall as a reminder to me that indeed I can't always decide what will happen to me, but I can decide what kind of attitude I will have. I would like to share this poem with you as you start your journey.

Attitude

The longer I live, the more I realize the impact of attitude on life.
Attitude, to me, is more important than facts.
It is more important than education, than money, than circumstances, than failures, than successes, than what other people think or say or do.
It is more important than appearances, giftedness or skill.
It will make or break a company, a church, a home.
The remarkable thing is we have a choice every day regarding the attitude we will embrace for that day.
We cannot change our past.
We cannot change the fact that people will act a certain way.
We cannot change the inevitable.
The only thing we can do is play on the one thing we do have and that is our attitude.
I am convinced that life is 10% what happens to me and 90% how I react to it.
And so it is with you; we are in charge of our attitudes.

With the right attitude you will find that life is a song and you'll sing it; a game and you'll play it. You'll meet life's challenges and discover a stronger sense of character. With a controlled attitude you'll discover that when life requires certain sacrifices, you'll be able to meet them. You'll begin to realize your dreams and find love in life and you'll truly enjoy it!

Indeed this is my wish for each and every one of you reading this book. My hope is that your journey through life be an incredible one and like all journeys, yours will begin with a single step. You took that first step when you picked up this book to read.

As I mentioned in the preface, it is my desire to inspire and motivate you on your way to the incredible life you deserve. As you read through the quotes, poems and stories in *Life's Incredible: 10 Key Steps,* I would like to encourage you to choose your favorites and highlight them so you can refer back easily when you feel you need an attitude boost, additional motivation or simply a bit of inspiration.

Here's a quote about attitude I especially like.

You've got to dance like nobody's watching and love like it's never going to hurt.

As I have previously mentioned, I've learned a lot about attitude through the books I've read and the people I've associated with. One of the most powerful quotes I've ever read concerning attitude was delivered by the great leader Mahatma Ghandi when he said:

Man often becomes what he believes himself to be. If I keep on saying that I cannot do a certain thing, it is possible that I may end by really becoming incapable of doing it. On the contrary, if I shall have the belief that I can do it, I shall surely acquire the capacity to do it, even if I may not have it at the beginning.

That is really a powerful thought and one that leads me to a story that was told by Tony Campolo when he spoke at the annual "Gathering of Men" held in Chattanooga in the mid '90s. The noted sociologist told this story and titled it:

The Last Day of School

It seems that there was a lady named Jean Thompson and when she stood in front of her fifth-grade class on the very first day of school in the fall, she told the children a lie. Like most teachers, she looked at her pupils and said that she loved them all the same and that she would treat them all alike. But that was impossible because there in front of her, slumped in his seat on the third row, was a boy named Teddy Stoddard.

Mrs. Thompson had watched Teddy the year before and noticed he didn't play well with the other children, that his clothes were unkempt and that he constantly needed a bath. Add to it the fact that Teddy was unpleasant.

It got to the point during the first few months that she would actually take delight in marking his papers with a broad red pen, making bold Xs and then marking the "F" at the top of the paper biggest of all.

Because Teddy was a sullen little boy, nobody else seemed to enjoy him either. At the school where Mrs. Thompson taught, she was required to review each child's records and because of things, put Teddy's off until last. But when she opened his file, she was in for a surprise.

His first-grade teacher wrote, "Teddy is a bright, inquisitive child with a ready laugh. He does work neatly and has good manners. He is a joy to be around."

His second-grade teacher wrote, "Teddy is an excellent student and is well-liked by his classmates but he is troubled because his mother has a terminal illness and life at home must be a struggle."

His third-grade teacher wrote, "Teddy continues to work hard but his mother's death has been hard on him. He tries to do his best but his father doesn't show much interest and his home life will soon affect him if some steps aren't taken."

Teddy's fourth-grade teacher wrote, "Teddy is withdrawn and doesn't show much interest in school. He doesn't have many friends and some-times sleeps in class. He is tardy and could become a problem."

By now Mrs. Thompson realized the problem but Christmas was com-ing fast. She had all she could do with the school play and all, until the day before the holidays began. On the last day before the vacation would begin, she was forced to focus on Teddy Stoddard. Her children brought her presents, all in gay ribbon and bright paper, except for Teddy's, which was clumsily wrapped in the heavy brown paper of a scissored grocery bag.

Mrs. Thompson took pains to open it in the middle of the other pre-sents and some of the children started to laugh when she found a rhine-stone bracelet, with some stones missing and a bottle of inexpensive perfume that was one-quarter full. She stifled the laughter when she exclaimed how pretty the bracelet was and put it on. She then dabbed some of the perfume on her wrists.

At the end of the day, as the other children joyously raced from the room, Teddy Stoddard stayed behind just long enough to say, "Mrs. Thompson, today you smelled just like my mom used to smell." As soon as Teddy left, Mrs. Thompson knelt at her desk and there, at the end of the last day of school before Christmas vacation, cried for at least an hour. On that very day she quit teaching reading and writing and speaking. Instead, she began to teach children. And Jean Thompson paid particular attention to one they called "Teddy."

As she worked with him, his mind seemed to come alive. The more she encouraged him, the faster he responded and on days that there would be an important test Mrs. Thompson would remember the perfume. By the end of the year, Teddy had become one of the smartest children in the class and...well, he had also become the "pet" of the teacher who had once vowed to love all her students exactly the same.

A year later she found a note under her door from Teddy, telling her that of all the teachers he'd had in elementary school, she was his favorite.

Six years went by before she got another note from Teddy. Then he wrote he had finished high school, third in his class, and she was still his favorite teacher of all time.

Four years after that she got another letter, saying that while things had been tough at times, he had stayed in school, had stuck with it and would graduate from college with the highest honors. He assured Mrs. Thompson she was still his favorite teacher.

Then four more years passed and yet another letter came. This time he explained that after he got his bachelor's degree, he decided to go a little farther. The letter explained that she was still his favorite teacher but that now his name was a little longer and the letter was signed, "Theodore F. Stoddard, M.D."

The story doesn't end there. You see, there was yet another letter that spring. Teddy said that he'd met this girl and was to be married. He explained that his father had died a couple of years before and he was wondering...well, if Mrs. Thompson might agree to sit in the pew usually reserved for the mother of the groom.

You'll have to decide yourself whether or not she wore that bracelet, the one with several rhinestones missing. But I bet on that special day, Jean Thompson smelled just like...well, just like she smelled many years before on the last day of school before the Christmas holidays began.

That is one of my favorite stories in this whole book and no matter how many times I read it, I doubt I will ever be able to get through it without tears. What a heartwarming story and what a great tribute to our teachers who have the power to impact and influence the young lives they touch in such a positive way.

People come into your life for a number of reasons. Sometimes it's as if you know they're meant to be there; at other times you realize their importance in your life after the fact. In either instance, they're there to serve some sort of purpose; teach you a lesson or help figure out who you are or who you want to become. You don't always know when these people will come into your life or who they may be but when you lock eyes with them, you know that every moment they will affect your life in some profound way.

At times things will happen to you that seem awful, painful or unfair but in reflection you are able to understand that without overcoming those obstacles you would never have realized your true potential, strength, will-power or heart.

Everything in life happens for a reason, not by chance or means of good luck. Illness, injury, love, lost moments of true greatness, and yes, even moments of sheer stupidity all occur to test the limits of your soul. Without these tests, life would be like a smoothly paved, straight, flat road to nowhere—safe and comfortable, but dull and utterly pointless. The people you meet affect your life.

The successes and downfalls that you experience create who you are and yes, even the bad experiences can be learned from. In fact, they are probably the most poignant and important ones. If someone hurts you, betrays you or breaks your heart, forgive them because they have helped you learn about trust and the importance of being cautious to whomever you open your heart to. If someone loves you, love them back unconditionally, not only because they love you, but because they are teaching you to love and open your heart and eyes to little things.

Make every day count. Appreciate every moment and take from it everything that you possibly can, for you may never be able to experience it again. Talk to people you have never talked to before and actually listen when they talk to you.

Let yourself fall in love. Set your sights high. Hold your head up because you have every right to do so. Tell yourself you're a great individual and believe in yourself, for if you don't believe in yourself, no one else will believe in you either.

Create your own life and then go out and live it! You are on your way to an incredible life not only for yourself but for those whom you affect. You will have a better life than you ever dreamed if you will remember that no matter how hard you may try, you won't always be able to determine your circumstances in life but you can always determine your attitude toward them! Your attitude is the single most important ingredient in a successful life because generally speaking life is 10% what happens to you and 90% how you react to it. Choose a positive attitude and look for the value in every situation. The choice to do that is demonstrated in a story that is told about Robert DeVincenzo, the great golfer.

It is said that once after winning a prestigious tournament, DeVincenzo accepted his check, smiled for the cameras and went to the clubhouse to prepare to leave. Later, as he walked alone to his car, he was approached by a young woman who congratulated him on his victory and then went on to tell him about her child who was seriously ill and near death, saying that she did not know how she would pay the bills.

DeVincenzo was touched by the story and took out a pen, endorsed the check and gave it to the woman saying, "Make some good days for the baby."

The next week as DeVincenzo was having lunch at a country club, a Professional Golf Association official came to his table saying, "Some of the boys in the parking lot last week told me you met a young woman there after you won that tournament." DeVincenzo nodded. "Well," said the official, "I have news for you. She's a phony. She has no sick baby. She's not even married. She fleeced you, my friend."

"You mean there is no baby who is dying?" said DeVincenzo.

"That's right," said the official.

"That's the best news I've heard all week," DeVincenzo said.

Indeed DeVincenzo not only demonstrated a winning attitude, but even more importantly, his story is a reminder to us all to keep everything in its proper perspective.

Another story that demonstrates the importance of choosing the significant over the less important things in life, although not as moving as the story of DeVincenzo, is told about an expert on time management who was speaking to a group of business students. To drive a point home, the expert used an illustration the students are most likely never to forget and after I share it with you, chances are you won't forget it either.

As this man stood in front of the group of high-powered overachievers, he said, "Okay, time for a quiz." Then he pulled out a one-gallon, wide-mouthed jar and set it on a table in front of him. He produced about a dozen fist-sized rocks and carefully placed them, one at a time, into the jar. When the jar was filled to the top and no more rocks would fit inside, he asked, "Is this jar full?"

Everyone in the class said, "Yes."

Then he asked, "Really?"

He reached under the table and pulled out a bucket of gravel. He dumped some of the gravel in and shook the jar causing pieces of gravel to work themselves down into the spaces between the big rocks. He smiled and asked the group once more, "Is the jar full?"

By this time the class was onto him. "Probably not," one of them answered.

"Good!" he replied.

He reached under the table and brought out a bucket of sand. He dumped the sand in and it went into all the spaces left between the rocks and the gravel. Once more he asked the question, "Is the jar full?"

"No!" the class shouted.

Once again he said, "Good!"

Then he grabbed a pitcher of water and began to pour it in until the jar was filled to the brim. He looked up at the class and asked, "What is the point of this illustration?"

One eager beaver raised his hand and said, "The point is, no matter how full your schedule is, if you try really hard, you can always fit some more things into it!"

"No," the speaker replied, "that's not the point."

What this illustration teaches us is that:

If you don't put the big rocks in first, you'll never get them in at all.

Now I have to ask you, "What are the 'big rocks' in your life?"

Are they:

Time with your loved ones?

Your faith, your education, your finances?

A cause you feel particularly strong about?

Teaching or mentoring others?

A project you would like to accomplish?

Whatever you answer, remember to put the "big rocks" in first or you'll never get them in at all. Therefore, tonight or in the morning when you are reflecting on this short story, ask yourself this question: "What are the 'big rocks' in my life?"

Then put those in your jar first.

When you understand what is most important in your life, you will be able to get your life in balance. With your life in balance, you'll be able to find what makes you happy. And what better time to decide to be happy than right now!

Unfortunately many of us continually postpone our happiness. It's not that we consciously set out to do so, but we keep convincing ourselves that indeed, "Someday I'll be happy." We tell ourselves we'll be happy when our bills are paid, when we get out of school, when we get our first job, get that big promotion. We convince ourselves that life will be better after we get married, have a baby; then another.

After that we find ourselves frustrated that the kids aren't old enough. We think we'll be more content when they are, only to discover that we're frustrated when we have teenagers to deal with. At this point we feel certain we'll be happy when they're out of that stage. We later tell ourselves that our life will be complete when our spouse gets his or her act together, when we get a nicer car, are able to go on a nice vacation, when we retire, and on and on.

The truth is, there is no better time to be happy than right now! If not now, when?

Our life will always be filled with challenges. It's best to admit this to ourselves and decide to be happy anyway.

Alfred D'Souza said, "For a long time it had seemed to me that life was about to begin—real life. But there was always some obstacle in the way, something to be gotten through first, some unfinished business, time still to be served, a debt to be paid. Then life would begin. At last it dawned on me that these obstacles were my life."

He goes on to say, "This perspective helps one to see that there is no way to happiness; happiness is the way. So, treasure every moment that you have and treasure it more because you share it with someone special; and remember that time waits for no one."

> ### *YESTERDAY IS HISTORY,*
> ### *TOMORROW IS A MYSTERY,*
> ### *TODAY IS A GIFT,*
> ### *THAT'S WHY IT'S CALLED THE PRESENT!*

So stop waiting until you finish school or go back to school;
Until you lose 10 pounds or gain 10 pounds;
Until you have kids or your kids leave the house;
Until you start work or retire;
Until you get married or divorced;
Until Friday night or Sunday morning;
Until you get a new car or home or until your car or home is paid off;
Until spring, summer, fall, or winter;
Until the first or fifteenth;
Until "your song" comes on;
Until you've had a drink or sobered up;
Until you die, until you are risen again.

Instead decide there is no better time to be happy than right now!

HAPPINESS IS A JOURNEY, NOT A DESTINATION.

For like D'Souza said, and my own dear dad just days before he passed away, "Time waits for no one." Make today the best day of your life because as the following prayer suggests, every day can be the best day of your life if you will stop and count your many blessings.

Today when I awoke, I suddenly realized that this is the best day of my life, ever!

There were times when I wondered if I would make it to this day; but I did and because I did, I'm going to celebrate!

Today I'm going to celebrate what an unbelievable life I have had so far; the accomplishments, the many blessings, and yes, even the hardships because they have served to make me stronger.

I will go through this day with my head held high and a happy heart. I will marvel at God's seemingly simple gifts: the morning dew, the sun, the clouds, the trees, the flowers, the birds. Today none of these miraculous creations will escape my notice.

Today I will share my excitement for life with other people. I'll make someone smile. I'll go out of my way to perform an unexpected act of kindness for someone I don't even know. Today I'll give a sincere compliment to someone who seems down. I'll tell a child how special he or she is and I'll tell someone I love just how deeply I care for them and how much they mean to me.

Today is the day I quit worrying about what I don't have and start being grateful for all the wonderful things God has already given me. I'll remember that to worry is just a waste of time because my faith in God and His divine plan ensures everything will be just fine.

And tonight before I go to bed, I'll go outside and raise my eyes to the heavens and stand in awe at the beauty of the stars and the moon and all the heavens. And I will praise God for these magnificent treasures.

As the day ends and I lay my head down on my pillow, I will thank the Almighty for the best day of my life and I will sleep the sleep of a contented child, excited with the expectation that tomorrow is going to be the best day of my life!

What a wonderful thought, "to sleep the sleep of a contented child." There is probably not a more comforting thought in the world, which brings me to a cute story about age. It seems age is a funny thing. Do you realize that the only time in our lives we like to get old is when we're kids? Think about it.

If you're younger than 10 years old, you're so excited about aging that you think in fractions. For instance, if someone asks your age you say, "I'm four and a half." (You would never say I'm 36 and a half!) But when we're four going on five it's a different story!

Then when you get into your teens, you can't hold back; you jump to the next number and when asked how old you are, you say, "I'm gonna be 16." Even if you're only 12, you're gonna be 16! Of course then comes the greatest day of your life and you become 21. Even the words sound like a ceremony, you *become* 21!

But then you turn 30, and what happens there? Suddenly it makes you sound like bad milk. "He *turned*; we had to throw him out; she's no fun now." What's wrong? What's changed? You *become* 21, you *turn* 30, but look out because soon you're *pushing* 40. Sounds like it's really slipping away now!

You *become* 21, you *turn* 30, you're *pushing* 40, but then, alas, you *reach* 50 and what? Are your dreams all gone or what?

Okay, so you think you've lost it all? Let's recap: you *become* 21, you *turn* 30, you're *pushing* 40, you *reach* 50, but then what happens? You *make it* to 60 and with a sigh of relief you say, "I didn't think I'd make it!" So you *become* 21, you *turn* 30, you're *pushing* 40, you *reach* 50, you *make it* to 60 and by this time you've built up so much speed, you *hit* 70!

After that, it's a day by day thing. After that you *hit* Wednesday, Thursday or Friday till you reach your 80s when you *hit* breakfast, lunch or dinner. If you're like my grandmother, you won't even buy green bananas professing, "It's an investment you know!"

It doesn't end there though. Once you're in your 90s, you start going backwards saying, "I was just 92." Then a strange thing happens if you make it past 100, you become a little kid again proudly saying, "I'm 100 and a half!" Kind of makes you wish you were six again, but that's in Chapter 2!

I love stories that demonstrate a winning attitude! The next story not only demonstrates a winning attitude but a winning spirit as well and it's one that's sure to inspire and motivate you.

A few years ago at the Seattle Special Olympics, nine contestants, all physically or mentally challenged, assembled at the starting line for the 100-yard dash. At the gun, they all started out, not exactly in a dash, but with a relish to run the race to the finish and win.

All, that is, except one boy who stumbled on the asphalt, tumbled over a couple of times and began to cry. The other eight heard the boy cry. They slowed down and looked back. They all turned around and went back. Every one of them. One girl with Downs syndrome bent down and kissed him and said, "This will make it better." All nine linked arms and walked across the finish line together.

Everyone in the stadium stood and the cheering went on for several minutes. People who were there are still telling the story. Why? Because deep down we know this one thing: What truly matters in this life is more than winning for ourselves. What truly matters is helping others win, even if it means slowing down and changing our course.

I remember the first time I read that story. It gave me goose bumps and caused tears to well up in my eyes. It still does. What an incredible story! What an incredible demonstration of the winning attitude. Indeed we can't always direct the winds, but we can adjust the sails.

Another expression I've often heard is that when life hands you lemons, you should make lemonade. I can recall thinking at one time, "Well that's a nice Pollyanna attitude, but it's not realistic." Since then I have found out differently. To turn the lemons in life into lemonade is the best thing we can do. It all starts with a positive attitude. Amazingly when I changed my attitude, my life began to change!

While I used to dwell on the fact that life had been less than fair to me, when I began counting my blessings, I soon realized how very much I had to be thankful for. And ultimately when I began giving thanks for what I already had, my blessings increased.

I encourage you to do what I did. Beginning tomorrow morning when the alarm clock goes off and you clutch your blanket and moan because you have to get up, count your blessings. Start with the fact that you can hear, for there are many who are deaf.

And then as you fight to keep your eyes closed against the morning light as long as possible, thank the Lord that you can see, for there are many who are blind.

And when you continue to lie in your bed and huddle, thank the Lord for the power to rise, for there are those who are bedridden and will never be able to get up.

Even though the first hour of the day seems more hectic than you can bear—when socks are lost, toast is burned, tempers are short and the children are loud—be thankful for your family. There are many who are lonely and have no family.

And even though your breakfast table never looks like the pictures in magazines and the menu is at times unbalanced, thank the Lord for the food you have. There are many who are hungry.

When the monotonous activities of your job begin to get to you, thank the Lord that you have a job, for there are many who are unemployed.

At times you'll wish your circumstances weren't so modest and bemoan your day-to-day fate; thank the Lord for life.

When it comes to attitude, what you choose to see often is what you get.

There is a lot to be said about attitude. Golfer Arnold Palmer has never flaunted his success. Although he has won hundreds of trophies and awards, the only trophy in his office is a battered little cup that he got for his first professional win at the Canadian Open in 1955.

In addition to the cup, he has a lone framed plaque on the wall. The plaque tells you why he has been successful on and off the golf course. It reads:

> If you think you are beaten, you are.
> If you think you dare not, you don't.
> If you think to win but think you can't,
> It's almost certain that you won't.
>
> Life's battles don't always go
> To the stronger woman or man,
> But sooner or later, those who win
> Are those who think they can.

Instead of focusing on the work to get to a desired destination, focus on the enjoyment you'll experience once you get there and the details, the obstacles and whatever challenges you may encounter will be easier to handle.

Sometimes the winning attitude is so subtle that it is virtually unnoticed as the following story will demonstrate.

In the fall of '96 my son and I were in Montreal on vacation. We were out shopping and I stopped to put a dollar in one of the shopping mall bag dispensers. When I attempted to pull the handles to release my bag, I realized they were tangled and as such I was unable to pull my bag up and out freely. As I worked to untangle the bags my son suggested I just give up and go to the information booth for a refund. I refused to do so and alas my persistence paid off and I was able to eventually slide my bag free. As I looked back at him and smiled with pride, he said, "Way to go Mom. You didn't give up." He knew. Small accomplishments lead to big successes. For me it was more than a shopping bag, it was a tradition. I collect shopping bags and since this was my first trip to Montreal, an Eaton Mall shopping bag was a must! Of course for my son retrieving a shopping bag was not a priority. The thing to recognize here is the fact that even in such a small accomplishment he was able to recognize a winning attitude.

The winning attitude is not something we're born with, but rather something we develop. My son had developed the winning attitude and so he recognized it. It's what enabled him to play championship tennis. It's what gave him the motivation to go on even when it seemed all was lost. It's what made him a winner even when the score wasn't in his favor. It's what gave him the drive to play when quitting would have been the easier option.

As triumphantly as I had pulled my shopping bag out that day, I recalled my son's triumph at a tennis tournament a few months earlier. It was an extremely hot summer day in southeast Texas and he had already played two tough matches. As he was about to play his third match he confided that his legs were beginning to cramp. Indeed I could see he was in pain and my heart ached for him as I sat in the stands and watched him play. I noticed the leg cramps getting worse and as he began holding his stomach I knew he was suffering from stomach cramps as well. Oh how I wanted to run out and pull him off the court, encourage him to just give it up, throw in the towel, admit he couldn't possibly win and it really wasn't worth the pain. Yes, that's what I wanted to do, but I knew I couldn't and I knew he'd never quit.

By the end of the match, he could barely move from one side of the court to the other and his serves, as well as his returns, lacked their usual power. In spite of the pain, he finished the match and no, the final score didn't show he had won, but to me as well as a number of people in the audience, he had indeed won. He had refused to give up. Winning is an attitude.

You too can develop the winning attitude. Following are 12 points on attitude. I urge you to read each of them for the next 21 days and see the difference they'll make in your life.

1. It is your attitude at the beginning of a task more than anything else that will determine your success or failure.

2. It is your attitude toward life that will determine life's attitude toward you. Despite many people's belief to the contrary, life plays no favorites.

3. You control your attitude. If you are negative it is because you have decided to be negative and not because of other people or circumstances.

4. Act as if you have a good attitude. Remember actions trigger feelings just as feelings trigger actions.

5. Before a person can achieve the results he wants, he must first become that person. He must then think, walk, talk, act and conduct himself in all of his affairs as would the person he wishes to become.

6. Treat everybody as the most important person in the world.

7. Attitudes are based on assumptions. In order to change attitudes one must first change one's assumptions.

8. Develop the attitude that there are more reasons why you should succeed than reasons why you should fail.

9. When you are faced with a problem, adopt the attitude that you can and will solve it.

10. We become what we think about. Control your thoughts and you will control your life.

11. Radiate the attitude of confidence, of well being, of a person who knows where he is going. You will then find good things happening to you right away.

12. In order to develop a good attitude, take charge first thing in the morning. Do you say, "Good morning, Lord" or "Good Lord, morning"?

Again I urge you to read these 12 points every day for 21 days and see how your life changes.

Feeling Creates Passion **II**

*To see the world in a grain of sand and heaven in a wildflower,
hold infinity in the palm of your hand and eternity in an hour.*

William Blake

There's an inspirational thought that is framed and sits amid the books on one of my shelves. Inscribed beneath an incredibly beautiful picture of a golf course that is obviously meant to stir the emotions is a quotation that reads:

There are many things in life that will catch your eye, but only a few will catch your heart; pursue them.

Indeed how often I have had this very thought!

What is it you feel passionate about? "Tell me where your heart is and I'll tell you who you are." I'm not sure where I first read that quote; maybe it's Shakespeare, maybe not. Regardless, there's a lot to be said for the statement and there's a wonderful story told about a man whose passion was a consuming desire to be an actor.

The young man wanted terribly to be an actor and all he needed was a part to play. Eventually his consuming desire to be an actor drew him to write his own part. He put together a script he was pleased with and began looking for someone to produce it for him. He went from agent to agent and studio to studio and was turned down over a thousand times. At this point even if he'd have given up, most people would have still considered him courageous. But he didn't and finally someone liked his script.

The timing couldn't have been better, for by now he was flat broke. He was offered $100,000 for the script but because the producer wanted someone else to play his part, he turned it down. His desire was to be an actor so he kept searching until he got exactly what he wanted.

He starred in the movie he'd written and won an Oscar for his performance. It was then followed by four sequels and because he held onto his dream, turning down the $100,000 buyout offer, he now gets several million per picture. What would have happened if Sylvester Stallone had avoided rejection? Nobody would have ever known who Rocky was.

Here's another heartwarming story that wonderfully demonstrates the opening quote. It's a story about a very wealthy man who, with his devoted young son shared a passion for art collecting. Together they traveled around the world, adding only the finest art treasures to their collection. Priceless works by Picasso, Van Gogh, Monet and many others adorned the walls of the family estate.

The widowed elder man looked on with satisfaction as his only child became an experienced art collector. The son's trained eye and sharp business mind caused his father to beam with pride as they dealt with art collectors around the world.

As winter approached, war engulfed the nation and the young man left to serve his country. After only a few short weeks, his father received a telegram. His beloved son was missing in action. The art collector anxiously awaited more news, fearing he would never see his son again. Within days, his fears were confirmed. The young man had died while rushing a fellow soldier to a medic.

Distraught and lonely, the old man faced the upcoming Christmas holidays with anguish and sadness. The joy of the season, a season that he and his son had so looked forward to, would visit his house no longer.

On Christmas morning, a knock on the door awakened the depressed old man. As he walked to the door, the masterpieces of art on the walls only reminded him that his son was not coming home. As he opened the door, he was greeted by a soldier with a large package in his hand. He introduced himself to the man by saying, "I was a friend of your son. I was the one he was rescuing when he died. May I come in for a few moments? I have something to show you."

As the two began to talk, the soldier told of how the man's son had told everyone of his, not to mention his father's love of fine art. "I'm an artist," said the soldier, "and I want to give you this." As the old man unwrapped the package, the paper gave way to reveal a portrait of the man's son. Though the world would never consider it the work of a genius, the painting featured the young man's face in striking detail. Overcome with emotion, the man thanked the soldier, promising to hang the picture above the fireplace.

A few hours later, after the soldier had departed, the old man set about his task. True to his word, the painting went above the fireplace, pushing aside thousands of dollars of paintings. And then the man sat in his chair and spent Christmas gazing at the gift he had been given.

During the days and weeks that followed, the man realized that even though his son was no longer with him, the boy's life would live on because of those he had touched. He would soon learn that his son had rescued dozens of wounded soldiers before a bullet stilled his caring heart. As the stories of his son's gallantry continued to reach him, fatherly pride and satisfaction began to ease the grief.

The painting of his son soon became his most prized possession, far eclipsing any interest in the pieces for which museums around the world clamored. He told his neighbors it was the greatest gift he had ever received.

The following spring, the old man became ill and passed away. The art world was in anticipation. With the collector's passing and his only son dead, those paintings would be sold at an auction.

According to the will of the old man, all of the art works would be auctioned on Christmas day, the day he had received his greatest gift. The day soon arrived and art collectors from around the world gathered to bid on some of the world's most spectacular paintings. Dreams would be fulfilled this day; greatness would be achieved as many would claim, "I have the greatest collection."

The auction began with a painting that was not on any museum's list. It was the painting of the man's son. The auctioneer asked for an opening bid. The room was silent. "Who will open the bidding with $100?" he asked. Minutes passed. No one spoke. From the back of the room came, "Who cares about that painting? It's just a picture of his son. Let's forget it and go on to the good stuff." More voices echoed in agreement. "No, we have to sell this one first," replied the auctioneer.

"Now who will take the son?" Finally, a friend of the old man spoke. "Will you take $10 for the painting? That's all I have. I knew the boy, so I'd like to have it. I have $10." "Will anyone go higher?" called the auctioneer. After more silence, the auctioneer said, "Going once, going twice. Gone." The gavel fell. Cheers filled the room and someone exclaimed, "Now we can get on with it and bid on these treasures!"

The auctioneer looked at the audience and announced the auction was over. Stunned disbelief quieted the room. Someone spoke up and asked, "What do you mean it's over? We didn't come here for a picture of some old guy's son. What about all of these paintings? There are millions of dollars of art here! I demand that you explain what's going on here!"

The auctioneer replied, "It's very simple. According to the will of the father, whoever takes the son gets it all."

I wonder, as you might, if there isn't perhaps a deeper message here? Could it be that just as the art collectors discovered on that Christmas day, so is it today? What a tremendously inspirational story, "Whoever takes the son, gets it all."

Beauty is not in the face; beauty is a light in the heart.
Love gives naught but itself and takes naught but from itself.
Love possesses not nor would it be possessed;
For love is sufficient unto love.

What a beautiful thought the above message offers, for beauty is a light in the heart. Have you ever wondered what it would be like to have the innocence, the wonder and excitement you had when you were a child? The next story suggests just what we might feel like if indeed we could be six again. It was shared with me by a friend of mine.

I Want to Be Six Again

I want to be six again.

I want to go to McDonald's and think it's the best place in the world to eat.

I want to sail sticks across a fresh mud puddle and make waves with the rocks.

I want to think M & M's are better than money 'cause you can eat them.

I want to play kickball during recess and stay up on Christmas Eve waiting to hear Santa and Rudolph on the roof.

I long for the days when life was simple. When all you knew were your colors, the addition tables, and simple nursery rhymes, but it didn't bother you because you didn't know what you didn't know and you didn't care.

I want to go to school and have snack time, recess, gym, and field trips.

I want to be happy because I don't know what should make me upset.

I want to think the world is fair, and everyone in it is honest and good.

I want to believe that anything is possible. At some time, while I was maturing, I learned too much. I learned of nuclear weapons, starving and abused kids, and unhappy marriages.

I want to be six again.

I want to think that everyone, including myself, will live forever because I don't know the concept of death.

I want to be oblivious to the complexity of life and be overly excited by the little things again.

I want television to be something I watch for fun, not something I use for escape from the things I should be doing.

I want to live knowing the little things I find exciting will always make me as happy as when I first learned them.

I want to be six again.

I remember not seeing the world as a whole but rather being aware of only the things that directly concerned me.

I want to be naive enough to think that if I'm happy, so is everyone else.

I want to walk down the beach and think only of the sand beneath my feet, and the possibility of finding that blue piece of sea glass I'm looking for.

I want to spend my afternoons climbing trees and riding my bike, letting the grownups worry about time, the dentist, and how to find the money to fix the car.

I want to wonder what I'll do when I grow up, not worry what I'll do if this doesn't work out.

I want that time back. I want to use it now as an escape, so that when my computer crashes, or I have a mountain of paperwork, or two depressed friends, or second thoughts about so many things, I can travel back and build a snowman without thinking about anything except whether the snow sticks together and what I can possibly use for the snowman's mouth.

I want to be six again.

To be six again, what a wonderful nostalgic thought! For me it evokes warm feelings, memories of summers on my grandparent's farm, with cool summer breezes wafting in my bedroom window. It's memories of a million or more stars twinkling in the heavens above and all the wishes made on them. It's being awoken by a rooster's crow instead of an alarm clock. It's racing to the pond in the pasture to cool off in the heat of the afternoon. It's evenings spent on the front porch swing, dreaming and planning our futures. We couldn't wait to get older then...and today we dream of being six again! What a joy to be young and what a blessing children are in our lives. We can learn a lot from children as the next story demonstrates.

It was only five days before Christmas. The spirit of the season hadn't yet caught up with me, even though cars packed the parking lot of every shopping center in the area. Inside the stores, it was worse as last minute shoppers scrambled to fill their shopping carts. As shoppers jammed the aisles, I wondered, "Why did I come today?" My feet ached almost as much as my head. My list contained names of several people who claimed they wanted nothing but I knew their feelings would be hurt if I didn't buy them something. Buying for someone who had everything and deploring the high cost of items, I considered gift-buying anything but fun. Hurriedly, I filled my shopping cart with last minute items and proceeded to the long checkout lines. I picked the shortest line possible but even so it looked as if it would mean at least a 20-minute wait.

In front of me were two small children, a boy of about 10 and a younger girl about 5. The boy wore a ragged coat with enormously large, tattered tennis shoes that jutted far out in front of his much-too-short jeans. He clutched several crumpled dollar bills in his grimy hands. The girl's clothing resembled her brother's. Her head was a matted mass of curly hair. Remainders of an evening meal showed on her small face. She carried a beautiful pair of shiny gold house slippers. As the Christmas music sounded in the store's stereo system, the girl hummed along off-key, but happily.

When we finally approached the checkout register, the girl carefully placed the shoes on the counter. She treated them as though they were a treasure. The clerk rang up the bill. "That will be $6.09," she said. The boy laid his crumpled dollars atop the stand while he searched his pockets. He finally came up with $3.12. "I guess we'll have to put them back," he bravely said. "We will come back some other time, maybe tomorrow." With that statement, a soft sob broke from the little girl. "But Jesus would have loved these shoes," she cried. "Well, we'll go home and work some more. Don't cry. We'll come back," he said.

Quickly I handed $3.00 to the cashier. These children had waited in line for a long time. And, after all, it was Christmas. Suddenly a pair of arms came around me and a small voice said, "Thank you, Sir."

"What did you mean when you said Jesus would like the shoes?" I asked. The small boy answered, "Our mommy is sick and is going to heaven. Daddy said she might go before Christmas to be with Jesus." The girl spoke, "My Sunday school teacher said the streets in heaven are shiny gold just like these shoes. Won't mommy be beautiful walking on those streets to match these shoes?"

My eyes flooded as I looked into her tear-streaked face. "Yes," I answered, "I am sure she will." Silently I thanked God for using these children to remind me of the true spirit of giving.

After all Christmas is not about the amount of money paid, nor the amount of gifts purchased, nor trying to impress friends and relatives. Christmas is about the love in your heart you're willing to share with others as the story so readily demonstrates. I have a motivational calendar that sits on my desk and one of my favorite quotes is:

> **IT'S NOT WHAT WE GIVE, BUT WHAT WE SHARE; FOR THE GIFT WITHOUT THE GIVER IS BARE.**

To emphasize that thought further, here is a poem by an unknown author I'd like to share with you. It's titled:

The Most Beautiful Flower

The park bench was deserted as I sat down to read,
beneath the long, straggly branches of an old willow tree.
Disillusioned by life with good reason to frown,
for the world was intent on dragging me down.

And if that weren't enough to ruin my day,
a young boy approached me, all tired from play.
He stood right before me with his head tilted down
and said with great excitement, "Look what I found!"

In his hand was a flower, and what a pitiful sight,
with its petal all worn—not enough rain or too little light.
Wanting him to take his dead flower and go off to play,
I faked a small smile and then shifted away.

But instead of retreating he sat next to my side
and declared with overacted surprise,
"It sure smells pretty and it's beautiful too.
That's why I picked it. Here, it's for you."

The weed before me was dying or dead,
not vibrant of colors; orange, yellow or red.
But I knew I must take it, or he might never leave.
So I reached for the flower, and replied, "Thanks, just what I need."

But instead of him placing the flower in my hand,
he held it in mid-air without reason or plan.
It was then that I noticed for the very first time
that weed-toting boy could not see; he was blind.

I heard my voice quiver, tears shone in the sun
as I thanked him for picking the very best one.
"You're welcome," he smiled, and then ran off to play,
unaware of the impact he'd had on my day.

I sat there and wondered how he managed to see
a self-pitying woman beneath an old willow tree.
How did he know of my self-indulged plight?
Perhaps from his heart, he'd been blessed with true sight.

Through the eyes of a blind child, at last I could see
the problem was not with the world, the problem was with me.
And for all those times, I myself had been blind,
I vowed to see the beauty in life, and appreciate every second that's
mine.

And then I held that wilted flower up to my nose
and breathed in the fragrance of a beautiful rose.
And I smiled as I watched that young boy, another weed in hand,
about to change the life of an unsuspecting old man.

What an incredible difference we can make in the lives of others. There's another warm story that beautifully demonstrates the sentiment that it's not what we give but what we share that makes a difference. I believe the events actually took place in New Orleans but could have occurred almost anywhere.

It was an unseasonably hot day. Everybody it seemed, was looking for some kind of relief, so an ice cream store was a natural place to stop.

A little girl, clutching her money tightly, entered the store. Before she could say a word, the store clerk sharply told her to get outside and read the sign on the door and stay out until she put on some shoes. She left slowly and a big man followed her out of the store.

He watched as she stood in front of the store and read the sign, "No bare feet." Tears started rolling down her cheeks as she turned and walked away. Just then the big man called to her. Sitting down on the curb, he took off his size 12 shoes, and set them in front of the girl saying, "Here, you won't be able to walk in these, but if you sort of slide along, you can get your ice cream cone."

Then he lifted the little girl up and set her feet into the shoes. "Take your time," he said. "I get tired of moving them around and it'll feel good to just sit here and eat my ice cream." The shining eyes of the little girl could not be missed as she shuffled up to the counter and ordered her ice cream cone.

He was a big man, all right. Big belly, big shoes, but most of all, he had a big heart.

Life is a succession of moments. To live each one is to succeed.
                                                                    Corita Kent

With the help of some of my friends, I have compiled a list of things we call:

If I Have Learned Anything...

I've learned that you can get by on charm for about 15 minutes. After that, you'd better know something.

I've learned that you shouldn't compare yourself to the best others can do, but to the best you can do.

I've learned that it's not what happens to people that's important. It's what they do about it.

I've learned that you can do something in an instant that will give you a heartache for life.

I've learned that no matter how thin you slice it, there are always two sides.

I've learned that regardless of your relationship with your parents, you miss them terribly after they're gone.

I've learned that it's taken me a long time to become the person I want to be.

I've learned that it's a lot easier to react than it is to think.

I've learned that you should always leave loved ones with loving words. It may be the last time you see them.

I've learned that you can keep going long after you think you can't.

I've learned that we are responsible for what we do, no matter how we feel.

I've learned that either you control your attitude or it controls you.

I've learned that regardless how hot and steamy a relationship is at first, the passion fades and there had better be something else to take its place.

I've learned that heroes are the people that do what has to be done when it needs to be done, regardless of the consequences.

I've learned that when the light turns green, you had better look both ways before proceeding.

I've learned that you can love someone and still not like him very much.

I've learned that there are people that love you dearly, but just don't know how to show it.

I've learned that your family won't always be there for you. It may seem funny, but people you aren't related to can take care of you and love you and teach you to trust people again. Families aren't biological.

I've learned that no matter how good a friend someone is, they're going to hurt you every once in a while and you must forgive them for that.

I've learned that it isn't always enough to be forgiven by others. Sometimes you have to learn to forgive yourself.

I've learned that no matter how bad your heart is broken, the world doesn't stop for your grief.

I've learned that our background and circumstances may have influenced who we are, but we are responsible for who we become.

I've learned that sometimes when my friends fight, I am forced to choose sides even when I don't want to.

I've learned that just because two people argue, it doesn't mean they don't love each other. And just because they don't argue, it doesn't mean they do.

I've learned that sometimes you have to put the individual above their actions.

I've learned that we don't have to change friends if we understand that friends change.

I've learned that two people can look at exactly the same thing and see something totally different.

I've learned that no matter how you try to protect your children they will eventually get hurt and you will hurt in the process.

I've learned that no matter how many friends you have, if you are their pillar, you will feel lonely and lost at the times you need them most.

I've learned that your life can be changed in a matter of hours by people who don't even know you.

I've learned that even when you think you have no more to give, when a friend cries out to you, you will find the strength to help.

I've learned that writing, as well as talking, can ease emotional pains.

I've learned that the paradigm we live in is not all that is offered to us.

I've learned that credentials on the wall do not make you a decent human being.

I've learned that people you care about most in life are taken from you too soon.

I've learned that my best friend and I can do anything or nothing and have the best time.

I've learned that sometimes the people you expect to kick you when you're down will be the ones to help you get back up.

I've learned that good quality underwear is worth the extra cost.

I've learned that I'm getting more and more like my mom, and I'm kinda happy about it.

I've learned that sometimes when I'm angry, I have the right to be angry but that doesn't give me the right to be cruel.

I've learned that true friendship continues to grow even over the longest distance. Same goes for true love.

I've learned that just because someone doesn't love you the way you want them to doesn't mean they don't love you with all they have.

I've learned that no matter how much I care, some people just don't care back.

I've learned that you should never tell a child that his dreams are unlikely or outlandish. Few things are more humiliating, and what a tragedy it would be if he believed it.

I've learned that I wish I could have told my parents that I love them one more time before they died.

I've learned that it takes years to build up trust and only seconds to destroy it.

I've learned that if you don't want to forget something, stick it in your underwear drawer.

I've learned that the clothes I like best are the ones with the most holes in them.

I've learned that you shouldn't be so eager to find out a secret. It could change your life forever.

I've learned that it's no fun putting on a wet swimsuit.

I've learned that it's not what you have in your life, but whom you have that counts.

I've learned that a good friend is better than a therapist.

I've learned that sandwiches cut diagonally taste better.

I've learned that you cannot make someone love you. All you can do is be someone who can be loved. The rest is up to them.

I've learned that it's hard to determine where to draw the line between being nice and not hurting people's feelings and standing up for what you believe.

I've learned that learning to forgive takes practice.

I've learned that money is a lousy way of keeping score.

I've learned that maturity has more to do with what types of experiences you've had and what you've learned from them and less to do with how many birthdays you've celebrated.

I've learned that there are many ways of falling and staying in love.

I've learned that although the word *love* can have many different meanings, it loses value when overly used.

I've learned that no matter the consequences, those who are honest with themselves get further in life.

I've learned that many things can be powered by the mind; the trick is self-control.

I've learned that love is not for me to keep, but to pass on to the next person.

I've learned that even if you do the right thing for the wrong reason, it's still the wrong thing to do.

And obviously we could go on and on with the list of things "I've learned" but instead of doing that, I'm going to add one last thought and then let you add your own life's lessons to the "I've learned" list we started.

When my children were babies, I couldn't wait for them to start walking and talking and anxiously helped them along. Of course when they had accomplished these skills, I then told them to sit quietly and not make so much noise! Fortunately, they didn't listen!

As they continued to grow up I soon found myself looking forward to the day they would start school only to find myself driving off in tears wondering where the first five years had gone. All too soon, they had passed through elementary, junior high and high school and it always seemed there were never enough hours in the day. Exhausted, I looked forward to graduation when things would "settle down." Needless to say, when the big day came I was ill prepared for the emptiness I felt and within a few short months, they were off to college—first my daughter and then my son.

I soon understood the term *empty nest syndrome* as I tried desperately to fill the void their leaving had left. Everything suddenly became a memento as I reminisced about the holidays, birthdays, summer vacations and special times we had shared. Suddenly the mundane everyday events had more meaning and I wondered what I might have missed while I was wishing my kids would hurry and grow up?

The following poem by an unknown author kind of sums up these feelings. I include it especially for all the young parents and future parents reading this book.

Oatmeal Kisses

One of these days you'll shout, "Why don't you kids grow up and act your age!" And they will. Or, "You guys get outside and find yourselves something to do and don't slam the door!" And they won't.

You'll straighten up their bedroom neat and tidy; bumper stickers discarded, bedspreads tucked and smooth, toys displayed on the shelves, hangers in the closet, animals caged, and you'll say out loud, "Now I want it to stay this way." And it will.

You'll prepare a perfect dinner with a salad that hasn't been picked to death and a cake with no finger traces in the icing and you'll say, "Now, there's a meal for company." And you'll eat it alone.

You'll say, "I want complete privacy on the phone. No dancing around. No demolition crews. Silence! Do you hear?" And you'll have it.

No more plastic tablecloths stained with spaghetti. No more bedspreads to protect the sofa from damp bottoms. No more gates to stumble over at the top of the steps. No more clothespins under the sofa. No more playpens to arrange a room around.

No more anxious nights under a vaporizer tent. No more sand on the sheets or Popeye movies in the bathrooms. No more iron-on patches, wet knotted shoestrings, tight boots or rubber bands for ponytails.

Imagine. A lipstick with a point on it. No baby-sitter for New Year's Eve. Washing only once a week. Seeing a steak that isn't ground. Having your teeth cleaned without a baby on your lap.

No PTA meetings. No car pools. No blaring radios. No one washing her hair at eleven o'clock at night. Having your own roll of Scotch tape.

Think about it. No more Christmas presents out of toothpicks and library paste. No more sloppy oatmeal kisses. No more tooth fairy. No giggles in the dark. No knees to heal, no responsibility.

Only a voice crying, "Why don't you grow up?" and the silence echoing, "I did."

As we reach the end of this chapter, I'd like to close with a dynamic quote by Paul D. Shafer and another poem by an unknown author.

The most important single influence in the life of a person is another person...who is worthy of emulation.

There are little eyes upon you and they're watching night and day,
There are little ears that quickly take in every word you say.

There are little hands all eager to do anything you do;
And little children dreaming of the day they'll be like you.

You're the little children's idol, you're the wisest of the wise.
In their little minds about you, no suspicions ever rise.

They believe in you devoutly, hold all you say and do;
They will say and do in your way when they're grown up just like you.

There's a wide-eyed little student who believes you're always right;
And their eyes are always opened and they watch you day and night.

You are setting an example every day in all you do;
For the little child who's waiting to grow up to be like you.

Understanding the Need to Be Flexible

III

*We cannot direct the wind,
but we can adjust the sails.*

There's a wonderful quote by one of my favorite authors, Norman Vincent Peale, that I have hanging on my refrigerator. Quite simply it says:

Change your thoughts and you change your world.

What a simple, yet profound idea. Another quote I've always enjoyed is, "What the mind of man can conceive and believe, it can achieve." The kind of life you will have will be determined in part by your thoughts. If you will have the "good life," you must first believe it will be yours.

There's a story told about an elderly man and his wife who entered the lobby of a small hotel in Philadelphia one stormy night many years ago. As the story goes, the couple was trying to get out of the rain and approached the front desk hoping to get some shelter for the night.

"Could you possibly give us a room here?" the husband asked. The clerk, a friendly man with a winning smile, looked at the couple and explained that there were three conventions in town. "All of our rooms are taken," the clerk said. "But I can't send a nice couple like you out in the rain at one o'clock in the morning. Would you perhaps be willing to sleep in my room? It's not exactly a suite, but it will be good enough to make you folks comfortable for the night." When the couple declined, the young man pressed on. "Don't worry about me; I'll make out just fine," the clerk told them. So the couple agreed.

As he paid his bill the next morning, the elderly man said to the clerk, "You are the kind of manager who should be the boss of the best hotel in the United States. Maybe someday I'll build one for you." The clerk looked at the couple and smiled. The three of them had a good laugh. As they drove away, the elderly couple agreed that the helpful clerk was indeed exceptional, as finding people who are both friendly and helpful isn't easy.

Two years passed. The clerk had almost forgotten the incident when he received a letter from the old man. It recalled that stormy night and enclosed a round-trip ticket to New York, asking the young man to pay them a visit. The old man met him in New York, and led him to the corner of Fifth Avenue and 34th Street. He then pointed to a great new building there, a palace of reddish stone, with turrets and watchtowers thrusting up to the sky.

"That," said the older man, "is the hotel I have just built for you to manage." "You must be joking," the young man said. "I can assure you that I am not," said the older man, a sly smile playing around his mouth.

The old man's name was William Waldorf Astor, and the magnificent structure was the original Waldorf-Astoria Hotel. The young clerk who became its first manager was George C. Boldt. This young clerk never foresaw the turn of events that would lead him to become the manager of one of the world's most glamorous hotels. But as a young hotel manager, he had gone above and beyond the usual duties; he had done what the following quote says:

Hold yourself responsible for a higher standard than anybody else expects of you.

What a beautiful thought and so fitting for the next story by an unknown author about an old fisherman.

Our house was directly across the street from the clinic entrance of Johns Hopkins Hospital in Baltimore. We lived downstairs and rented the upstairs rooms to outpatients at the clinic.

One summer evening as I was fixing supper, there was a knock at the door. I opened it to see a truly awful-looking man. "Why, he's hardly taller than my eight-year-old," I thought as I stared at the stooped, shriveled body. But the appalling thing was his face, which was all lopsided from swelling, red and raw. Yet his voice was pleasant as he said, "Good evening. I've come to see if you've a room for just one night. I came for a treatment this morning from the eastern shore and there's no bus 'til morning."

He told me he'd been hunting for a room since noon but with no success; no one seemed to have room. "I guess it's my face. I know it looks terrible, but my doctor says with a few more treatments..." For a moment I hesitated, but his next words convinced me. "I could sleep in this rocking chair on the porch. My bus leaves early in the morning."

I told him we would find him a bed, but to rest on the porch. I went inside and finished getting supper. When we were ready, I asked the old man if he would join us. "No thank you. I have plenty." And he held up a brown paper bag.

When I had finished the dishes, I went out on the porch to talk with him a few minutes. It didn't take a long time to see that this old man had an oversized heart crowded into that tiny body. He told me he fished for a living to support his daughter, her five children and her husband who was hopelessly crippled from a back injury. He didn't tell it by way of complaint; in fact, every other sentence was prefaced with a thanks to God for a blessing. He was grateful that no pain accompanied his disease, which was apparently a form of skin cancer. He thanked God for giving him the strength to keep going.

At bedtime, we put a camp cot in the children's room for him. When I got up in the morning, the bed linens were neatly folded and the little man was out on the porch. He refused breakfast, but just before he left for his bus, haltingly, as if asking a great favor, he said, "Could I please come back and stay the next time I have a treatment? I won't put you out a bit. I can sleep fine in a chair." He paused a moment and then added, "Your children made me feel at home. Grown-ups are bothered by my face, but children don't seem to mind."

I told him he was welcome to come again. And on his next trip he arrived a little after seven in the morning. As a gift he brought a big fish and a quart of the largest oysters I had ever seen. He said he had shucked them that morning before he left so that they'd be nice and fresh. I knew his bus left at 4:00 a.m. and I wondered what time he had to get up in order to do this for us.

In the years he came to stay overnight with us there was never a time that he did not bring us fish or oysters or vegetables from his garden. Other times we received packages in the mail, always by special delivery—fish and oysters packed in a box of fresh young spinach or kale, every leaf carefully washed. Knowing that he must walk three miles to mail these, and knowing how little money he had, made the gifts doubly precious. When I received these little remembrances, I often thought of a comment our next-door neighbor made after he left that first morning. "Did you keep that awful-looking man last night? I turned him away! You can lose roomers by putting up such people!" Maybe we did lose roomers once or twice. But oh, if only they could have known the old fisherman, perhaps their illness would have been easier to bear.

I know our family will always be grateful to have known him; from him we learned what it was to accept the bad without complaint and the good with gratitude to God.

Recently I was visiting a friend who has a greenhouse. As she showed me her flowers, we came to the most beautiful one of all, a golden chrysanthemum, bursting with blooms. But to my great surprise, it was growing in an old dented, rusty bucket. I thought to myself, "If this were my plant, I'd put it in the loveliest container I had!"

My friend changed my mind. "I ran short of pots," she explained, "and knowing how beautiful this one would be, I thought it wouldn't mind starting out in this old pail. It's just for a little while, until I can put it out in the garden."

She must have wondered why I laughed so delightedly, but I was imagining just such a scene in heaven. "Here's an especially beautiful one," God might have said when he came to the soul of the sweet old fisherman. "He won't mind starting in this small body." All this happened long ago and now in God's garden, how tall this lovely soul must stand.

A story that was told by our pastor recently makes a similar statement in that, "The Lord does not look at the things man looks at. Man looks at the outward appearance, but the Lord looks at the heart" (1 Samuel 16:7).

His name was John. He had wild hair, wore a T-shirt with holes in it and no shoes. This had literally been his wardrobe for his entire four years of college. He was brilliant, kind of esoteric and very, very bright. He became a Christian while attending college. Across the street from the campus was a well-dressed, very conservative church. They wanted to develop a ministry to the students, but were not sure how to go about it. One day John decided to go there.

He walked in with no shoes, jeans, his T-shirt and wild hair. The sermon had already begun so John started down the aisle looking for a seat. The church was completely packed and he couldn't find a seat. By now people were looking a bit uncomfortable, but no one said anything. John got closer and closer and closer to the pulpit and when he realized there were no seats, he just squatted down right on the carpet. (Although perfectly acceptable behavior at a college fellowship, trust me, this had never happened in this church before!)

By now the people were really uptight, and the tension in the air was thick. About this time the minister realized that from way at the back of the church, a deacon was slowly making his way toward John. Now the deacon was in his 80s, had silver-gray hair, a three-piece suit and a pocket watch. A godly man, very elegant, very dignified, very courtly; he walked with a cane and as he started walking toward this boy, everyone was saying to themselves, "You can't blame him for what he's going to do. How can you expect a man of his age and background to understand some college kid on the floor?"

It took a long time for the man to reach the boy. The church was utterly silent except for the clicking of the man's cane. All eyes were focused on him. You couldn't even hear anyone breathing. The people were thinking, "The minister can't even preach the sermon until the deacon does what he has to do."

And then they saw this elderly man drop his cane on the floor. With great difficulty he lowered himself and sat down next to John and worshipped with him so he wouldn't be alone. Everyone choked up with emotion. When the minister gained control he said, "What I'm about to preach you will never remember. What you have just witnessed, you will never forget."

What a dramatic lesson the deacon demonstrated in flexibility, which does sometimes require both strength and courage.

It takes strength to be firm and courage to be gentle.
It takes strength to stand guard and courage to let down your guard.
It takes strength to conquer and courage to surrender.
It takes strength to be certain and courage to have doubt.
It takes strength to fit in and courage to stand out.
It takes strength to feel a friend's pain and courage to feel
your own pain.
It takes strength to hide your own pain and courage to show it.
It takes strength to endure abuse and courage to stop it.
It takes strength to stand alone and courage to lean on another.
It takes strength to love and courage to be loved.
It takes strength to survive and courage to live.

Yes, it takes strength to survive and courage to live. So many times we sell ourselves short, and settle for surviving when we could truly be living. When I was a young mother I considered myself hard-working and ambitious. I cared for a home and two small children, served my church and community, and worked a full-time job. I met any challenge that was handed to me, on the job or in my personal life. Often I would crawl in bed exhausted at the end of the day. There were times when a bedtime story put me to sleep before it did my children. There were times I didn't have the energy to do the things with them they wanted me to do. Still I felt good about my life and proud of my accomplishments. I rationalized the fact that my children were too young to understand how hard I worked. One night, though, my six-year-old opened my eyes with a lesson I will never forget.

"Look, mom!" cried my daughter, pointing to a seagull swooping down for a morsel of food.

"Uh huh," I murmured matter of factly.

"Mom, can we have breakfast for supper tonight please?" she now asked.

"Yes, Rhonda," I answered without really even hearing what she had said.

Dinner, baths, laundry and work from the office all filled the hours until bedtime.

I settled her little brother in bed and then went up to tuck her in. Following prayers and a good night kiss, I was about to turn the light out when she stopped me.

"Mom, I forgot something."

"What now Rhonda," I asked impatiently.

"I have something for you," she said.

"Save it for tomorrow morning, okay, hon. I'm too tired tonight."

I could see disappointment on her freckled little face as she stuck out her lip and said, "Tonight you're too tired, tomorrow, you'll be too busy."

"I will take time." I promised her. Her words stung but I was too tired to argue so with a flip of the switch, I closed the door and headed back downstairs.

In the morning when I went in to awaken her for school, clutched in her chubby little fingers was the note she had wanted to give me the night before. I took the wadded piece of paper from her little hand. She had written, "To the best mom in the world. I love you because no matter how busy you may be, you always take time out to be with me."

My heart filled with love for this child of mine and the wisdom of her words. Funny how sometimes, as my parents used to say, "we can't see the forest for the trees." Her simple words were my reminder to look beyond the trees of life and see the beauty of the forest within, and from that day forward I tried to do just that. Several years later, I received a note from Rhonda. I now proudly share it with you.

Mom, you always seem to know the right thing to say and do.
No matter where I am, I know I can count on you.
There's never a problem I can't tell you about.
You give me support and confidence without doubt.
I'm glad I can share my thoughts and feelings with you.
You're my best friend, mom...I love you.
                                        Love forever,
                                        Rhonda
                                        Nov. 1986

And now a little story for all you guys reading this.

A man came home from work late again, tired and irritated to find his five-year-old son waiting for him at the door. "Daddy, may I ask you a question?" "Yeah, sure. What is it?" replied the man.

"Daddy, how much money do you make an hour?" "That's none of your business! What makes you ask such a thing?" the man said angrily. "I just want to know. Please tell me, how much do you make an hour?" pleaded the little boy.

"If you must know, I make $20 an hour." "Oh," the little boy replied, head bowed. Looking up, he said, "Daddy, may I borrow $10 please?" The father was furious. "If the only reason you wanted to know how much money I make is just so you can borrow some money to buy a silly toy or some other nonsense, then you march yourself straight to your room and go to bed. Think about why you're being so selfish. I work long, hard hours every day and don't have time for such childish games."

The little boy quietly went to his room and shut the door. The man sat down and started to get even madder about the little boy's questioning. How dare he ask such questions only to get some money! After an hour or so the man had calmed down and started to think he may have been a little hard on his son. Maybe there was something he really needed to buy with that $10 and he really didn't ask for money very often.

The man went to the door of the little boy's room and opened the door. "Are you asleep son?" he asked. "No, daddy, I'm awake," replied the boy. "I've been thinking, maybe I was too hard on you earlier," said the man. "It's been a long day and I took my aggravation out on you. Here's that $10 you asked for."

The little boy sat straight up, beaming. "Oh, thank you, daddy!" he yelled. Then, reaching under his pillow, he pulled out some more crumpled up bills. The man, seeing that the boy already had money, started to get angry again. The little boy slowly counted out his money, then looked up at the man. "Why did you want more money if you already had some?" the father grumbled.

"Because I didn't have enough, but now I do," the little boy replied. "Daddy, I have $20 now. Can I buy an hour of your time?"

Wow, what an incredible impact children can have on our lives!

I love this chapter! Once you learn the key step of flexibility, it will seem as if a whole new world has opened to you.

I also love the beach. It is one of my favorite places for relaxation and inspiration. There is a lot to be learned from the sea and in a chapter that deals with understanding the need to be flexible, what better story to share than that of the oyster?

There Once Was an Oyster

There once was an oyster whose story I tell,
who found that some sand had got in his shell.
It was only a grain, but it gave him great pain,
for oysters have feelings although they're so plain.

Now, did he berate the harsh workings of fate
that had brought him to such a deplorable state?
Did he curse at the government, cry for election
and claim that the sea should have given him protection?

No, he said to himself as he lay on a shell,
since I cannot remove it, I shall try to improve it.
Now the years have rolled 'round as the years always do,
and he came to his ultimate destiny, stew.

And the small grain of sand that had bothered him so
was a beautiful pearl all richly aglow.
Now the tale has a moral, for isn't it grand
what an oyster can do with a morsel of sand?
What couldn't we do if we'd only begin
with some of the things that get under our skin.

What a wonderful life you'll have once you start practicing the key step of flexibility! As you learn to relax, even the challenges and obstacles of life will be easier to handle. You won't understand everything. In fact some things will seem to make even less sense than before. What you will have though, is the freedom to show your feelings and when you're happy, you'll enjoy it; and when you're not, you'll deal with it. As you work to make things better, you won't feel the need to take the weight of the world on your shoulders. Taking one day at a time, you'll look forward to the future with hope and excitement. You'll accept the past without feeling guilty; what's done is done. You will never be alone; there will always be someone there for you to reach out to. You can have an incredible life! Dream, believe, love. With a willingness to do what it takes, your dreams will become your reality and the world will be your oyster.

It's never too late in fiction or in life to revise.

Nancy Thayer

The next story, which was shared with me by a friend of mine, is one of those life's lessons stories that is sure to stir the emotions and will most likely bring a tear to your eye as your heart wells up in compassion. It's the story of Jake.

Bill Andrews was a big, awkward, homely guy. He dressed oddly with ill-fitting clothes. There were several fellows who thought it smart to make fun of him. One day one fellow noticed a small tear in Bill's shirt and gave it a small rip. Another worker in the factory added his bit, and before long there was quite a ribbon dangling. Bill went on about his work and as he passed too near a moving belt the shirt strip was sucked into the machinery. In a split second the sleeve and Bill were in trouble. Alarms were sounded, switches pulled and trouble was avoided. The foreman, however, aware of what had happened, summoned the men and related this story:

In my younger days I worked in a small factory. That's where I first met Mike Havoc. He was big and witty, was always making jokes playing little pranks. Mike was a leader. Then there was Pete Lumas. He always went along with Mike. He was a follower. And then I remember Jake.

He was a little older than the rest of us—quiet, harmless, apart. He ate his lunch by himself. He wore the same patched trousers for three years straight. He never entered into the games we played at noon—wrestling, horseshoes and such. He was indifferent.

Jake was a natural target for practical jokes. He might find a live frog in his dinner pail or a dead rodent in his hat, but he always took it in good humor.

Then one fall when things were slack, Mike took off a few days to go hunting. Pete went along, of course. And they promised all of us that if they got anything they'd bring us each a piece. So we were all quite excited when we heard that they'd returned and that Mike had gotten a really nice big buck.

We heard more than that. Pete could never keep anything to himself and it leaked out that they had a real whopper to play on Jake. Mike had cut up the critter and had made a nice package for each of us. And for the laugh, for the joke of it, he had saved the ears, the tail, the hooves and it would be so funny when Jake unwrapped them.

Mike distributed his packages during the noon hour. We each got a nice piece, opened it and thanked him. The biggest package of all he saved until last. It was for Jake. Pete was all but bursting and Mike looked very smug. Like always, Jake sat by himself; he was on the far side of the big table.

Mike pushed the package over to where he could reach it, and we all sat and waited. Jake was never one to say much. You might never know that he was around for all the talking he did. In three years he'd never said a hundred words. So we were all quite hypnotized with what happened next.

He took the package firmly in his grip and rose slowly to his feet. He smiled broadly at Mike and it was then that we noticed his eyes were glistening. His Adam's apple bobbed up and down for a moment and then he got control of himself.

"I knew you wouldn't forget me," he said gratefully. "I knew you'd come through! You're big and you're playful but I knew all along that you had a good heart." He swallowed again and then took in the rest of us.

"I know I haven't seemed too chummy with you men, but I never meant to be rude. You see, I've got nine kids at home and a wife that's been an invalid, bedfast now for four years. She ain't ever going to get any better. And sometimes when she's real bad off, I have to sit up all night to take care of her. And most of my wages have had to go for doctors and medicine. The kids do all they can to help out, but at times it's been hard to keep food in their mouths. Maybe you think that it's funny that I go off by myself to eat my dinner. Well, I guess I've been a little ashamed because I don't always have anything between my bread. Or like today, maybe there's only a raw turnip in my pail. But I want you to know that this meat really means a lot to me. Maybe more than to anybody here because tonight my kids," he wiped the moisture from his eyes with the back of his hand, "...tonight my kids will have a really..." He tugged at the string.

We'd been watching Jake so intently we hadn't paid much notice to Mike and Pete. But we all noticed them now, because they both dove at once to try to grab the package. But they were too late. Jake had broken the wrapper and was already surveying his present. He examined each hoof, each ear and then he held up the tail. It wiggled limply. It should have been so funny but nobody laughed; nobody at all. But the hardest part was when Jake looked up and tried to smile.

This was where the foreman left the story and the men. He didn't need to say anymore but it was gratifying to notice that as each man ate his lunch that day, he shared part with Bill Andrews and one fellow even offered him his shirt.

Most great men and women are not perfectly rounded in their personalities, but are instead people whose one driving enthusiasm is so great it makes their faults seem insignificant.

Charles A. Cerami

> *TO THE WORLD YOU MIGHT BE ONE PERSON,*
> *BUT TO ONE PERSON, YOU MIGHT BE THE*
> *WORLD.*

Make Each Day of Your Life Happier

Share a kind word with a friend.

Give away a smile.

Tell one secret.

Listen to what someone has to say.

Listen with your heart to what someone cannot say.

Try one new thing.

Forgive one person who has hurt you.

Forgive yourself for past mistakes.

Realize your imperfections.

Discover your possibilities.

Make a new friend.

Accept responsibility for everything you do.

Refuse responsibility for anyone else's actions.

Dream one dream.

Watch the sunset.

Cherish what you have.

Cherish who you are.

Love your life.

Now go back and highlight the above list. It's such a simple recipe for happiness, you might easily overlook it.

And when you come to life's crossroads and view what you think is the end, remember God has a much wider vision and He knows it's only a bend. The road will go on and get smoother and after you've stopped for a rest, the path that lies hidden beyond you is often the part that is best. So rest and relax and grow stronger; let go and let God share your load and have faith in a brighter tomorrow. You've just come to a bend in the road. You're on your way to an incredible life!

It is the nature of man to rise to greatness if greatness is expected of him.

John Steinbeck

That is one of my favorite quotes! I could easily end this chapter with that, but according to my notes I should include a prescription for serenity. It begins with one of my dad's favorite sayings and ends with my mom's favorite prayer.

Prescription for Serenity

No one ever gets out of this world alive. Resolve therefore to maintain a sense of values.

Take care of yourself. Good health is everyone's major source of wealth. Without it serenity is harder to attain.

Resolve to be cheerful and helpful. People will repay in kind more often than not.

Avoid zealots. They are generally humorless.

Resolve to listen more and talk less. Rarely does anyone learn anything while talking.

Be wary of giving advice. The wise don't need it and the fools won't heed it.

Resolve to be tender with the young, compassionate with the aged, sympathetic with the striving, and tolerant of the weak and the wrong. Sometime in life you will have been all of these.

Do not equate money with success. The world abounds with big money makers who are miserable failures as human beings. What counts most about success is how a person achieves it.

Acknowledge lust when you feel it, but don't confuse it with love.

Don't take yourself too seriously. Humanity's saving grace is its sense of humor.

Set goals for yourself. Work hard to achieve them, but don't feel guilty if you don't. The hard work was your reward, not the achievement.

Learn to understand the Serenity Prayer:

God grant me the serenity to accept the things I cannot change, the courage to change the things I can and the wisdom to know the difference.

Loving Is the Key to Living IV

*No love, no friendship can cross the path of our destiny
without leaving some mark on it forever.*

Francois Mauriac

I have several motivational calendars around my house and office, on desks, countertops, wherever, all with different thoughts. One of the calendars was given to me by a good friend of mine and is titled, "A Friend Like You." The January 10 thought is:

> *Do not keep the alabaster boxes of your love and tenderness sealed up until your friends are dead. Fill their lives with sweetness. Speak approving, cheering words while their ears can hear them and while their hearts can be thrilled and made happier by them.*
> George William Childs

There's a story from an unknown source I would like to share now.

Once upon a time, there was an island where all the feelings lived: Happiness, Sadness, Knowledge, and all of the others including Love. However, one day it was announced to the feelings that the island would sink, so all prepared their boats and left. Love was the only one who stayed. Love wanted to stay until it started sinking.

When Love was almost sinking, he decided to ask for help. Richness was passing by Love in a beautiful boat. Love said, "Richness, can you take me with you?"

Richness answered, "No, I can't. There is a lot of gold and silver in my boat. There is no place here for you."

Love decided to ask Vanity who was also passing by, "Vanity, please help me!" "I can't help you Love. You are all wet and can probably damage my boat," Vanity answered.

Sadness was close by so Love asked for help. "Sadness, let me go with you." "Oh, Love, I am so sad that I prefer to go alone."

Happiness passed by Love too, but she was so happy that she did not listen when Love called her.

Suddenly, there was a voice, "Come, Love, I will take you." It was an elder. Love became very happy that he even forgot to ask the name of the elder. When they arrived to the other side, Love asked Knowledge who the elder was.

"It was Time."

"Time? But why did Time help me?"

"Because only Time is capable of understanding how great Love is," replied the elder.

A bell is not a bell until you ring it.
A song is not a song until you sing it.
Love in your heart wasn't put there to stay.
Love isn't love until you give it away!

A few months back, I left my office with every intention of visiting my dad sometime during the day. Because of Alzheimer's, dad had been confined to a nursing home for almost three years. Although I tried to see him several times a week, sometimes it was a challenge with my schedule.

This was one of those days. It seemed the more I tried to hurry, the farther behind I got. I entertained the idea of postponing the visit until the following morning. All day though I was haunted by a nagging feeling that I needed to go see him and by mid afternoon, I was sitting on the end of his bed visiting with him. We chatted as usual and then watched part of his favorite television program, "Judge Judy." He chuckled at her verdict as we both agreed she definitely "told it like it was." There was no pulling the wool over her eyes just as it had never been with dad!

As I prepared to leave, I gave him my usual hug, though he seemed to hug me back a bit longer than usual. When I kissed him on the cheek and told him I loved him, he said, "I love you too, Elizabeth Ann." When I said I'd see him for ice cream Sunday, he just smiled.

Exactly 12 hours later, my phone rang. There wouldn't be any more hugs, kisses or shared moments. There wouldn't be any more visits to Dairy Queen for ice cream on Sunday afternoon. My dad had passed away in his sleep.

I will forever be thankful that I made time for dad that day. When I was in school, the nuns that taught us would always tell us about our guardian angels and how we each had an angel to watch over us. Perhaps the inner voice I heard that day was my angel. Regardless I am glad I listened. When one of my friends heard what had happened, she sent me the following story about angels to share with you.

Barefoot and dirty, the girl just sat and watched the people go by. She never tried to speak, she never said a word. Many people passed, but never did one person stop.

It just so happens that the next day I decided to go back to the park, curious to see if the little girl would still be there. Right in the very spot as she had been the day before, she sat perched on high, with the saddest look in her eyes.

Today I decided to make my own move and walk over to her. As we all know, a park full of strange people is not a place for young children to play alone. As I began walking toward her, I could see the back of the little girl's dress indicated a deformity. I figured that was the reason people just passed by and made no effort to help.

As I got closer, the little girl slightly lowered her eyes to avoid my intent stare. I could see the shape of her back more clearly. It was grotesquely shaped in a humped-over form. I smiled to let her know it was okay. I was there to help, to talk.

I sat down beside her and opened with a simple "Hello." The little girl acted shocked and stammered a "Hi" after a long stare into my eyes.

I smiled and she shyly smiled back. We talked 'til darkness fell and the park was completely empty. Everyone was gone and we at once were alone. I asked the girl why she was so sad. The little girl looked at me and with a sad face said, "Because I'm different." I immediately said, "That you are!" and smiled. The little girl acted even sadder and said, "I know."

"Little girl," I said, "you remind me of an angel, sweet and innocent." She looked at me and smiled, slowly she stood to her feet and said, "Really?"

"Yes, dear, you're like a little guardian angel sent to watch over all those people walking by." She nodded her head "yes" and smiled and with that she spread her wings and said, "I am. I'm your guardian angel," with a twinkle in her eye.

I was speechless, surely I was seeing things. She said, "For once you thought of someone other than yourself. My job here is done." Immediately I stood to my feet and said, "Wait, so why did no one stop to help an angel?"

She looked at me and smiled, "You're the only one who could see me and you believed it in your heart." And she was gone. And with that my life was changed dramatically. So, when you think you're all you have, remember, your angel is always watching over you. Mine was.

Indeed it could have been my guardian angel that day urging me to make the time to see dad. What a huge difference one day would have made! I urge you, don't put off that "I love you" until tomorrow for tomorrow may be too late. There's a poem by an unknown author that does a wonderful job of getting this message across.

To love is one thing,
To be loved is another,
But to love and be loved...is everything.

Today

Yesterday I met a stranger...Today this stranger is my friend.
Had I not taken the time to say hello, or return a smile, or shake a hand.
or listen,
I would not have known this person.
Yesterday would have turned into today
and our chance of meeting would be gone.

Yesterday I hugged someone very dear to me.
Today they are gone...
and tomorrow will not bring them back.
Wouldn't it be nice if we all knew tomorrow would be here?
But this is not to be, so take the time TODAY
To give a hug, a smile, an "I love you."

In Chapter II, I alluded to a quote and at the time was not sure of its author. Although the words I used may not have been exact, the author of the quote, Houssaye, is noted in the following story from an unknown source.

John Blanchard stood up from the bench, straightened his Army uniform, and studied the crowd of people making their way through Grand Central Station.

He looked for the girl whose heart he knew, but whose face he didn't—the girl with the rose. His interest in her had begun 13 months before in a Florida library. Taking a book off the shelf he found himself intrigued, not with the words of the book, but with the notes penciled in the margin. The soft handwriting reflected a thoughtful soul and insightful mind.

In the front of the book, he discovered the previous owner's name, Miss Hollis Maynell. With time and effort he located her address. She now lived in New York City. He wrote her a letter introducing himself and inviting her to correspond. The next day he was shipped overseas for service in World War II.

During the next year and one month the two grew to know each other through the mail. Each letter was a seed falling on a fertile heart. A romance was budding.

Blanchard requested a photograph, but she refused. She felt that if he really cared, it wouldn't matter what she looked like.

When the day finally came for him to return from Europe, they scheduled their first meeting at 7:00 p.m. at the Grand Central Station in New York.

"You'll recognize me," she wrote, "by the red rose I'll be wearing on my lapel."

So at seven o'clock he was in the station looking for a girl whose heart he loved, but whose face he'd never seen.

Mr. Blanchard tells the story. A young woman was coming toward me, her figure long and slim. Her blonde hair lay back in curls from her delicate ears; her eyes were blue as flowers. Her lips and chin had a gentle firmness and in her pale green suit she was like springtime come alive.

I started toward her, entirely forgetting to notice that she was not wearing a rose. As I moved, a small, provocative smile curved her lips. "Going my way, sailor?" she murmured.

Almost uncontrollably I made one step closer to her and then I saw Hollis Maynell. She was standing almost directly behind the girl. A woman well past 40, who had graying hair tucked under a worn hat. She was more than plump, her thick-ankled feet thrust into low-heeled shoes.

The girl in the green suit was walking quickly away. I felt as though I was split in two, so keen was my desire to follow her, and yet so deep was my longing for the woman whose spirit had truly companioned me and upheld my own. And there she stood. Her pale, plump face was gentle and sensible, her gray eyes had a warm and kindly twinkle. I did not hesitate. My fingers gripped the small worn blue leather copy of the book that was to identify me to her.

This would not be love, but it would be something precious, something perhaps even better than love, a friendship for which I had been and must ever be grateful.

I squared my shoulders and saluted and held out the book to the woman, even though while I spoke I felt choked by the bitterness of my disappointment. "I'm Lieutenant John Blanchard, and you must be Miss Maynell. I am so glad you could meet me. May I take you to dinner?"

The woman's face broadened into a tolerant smile. "I don't know what this is about, son," she answered, "but the young lady in the green suit who just went by begged me to wear this rose on my coat. And she said if you were to ask me out to dinner, I should tell you that she is waiting for you at the big restaurant across the street. She said it was some kind of test!"

It's not difficult to understand and admire Miss Maynell's wisdom. As I mentioned in Chapter I, sometimes people will come into your life and you will know right away that they were meant to be there, to serve some purpose, teach you a lesson or help you figure out who you want to become.

The true nature of a heart is seen in its response to the unattractive. "Tell me whom you love," Houssaye wrote, "And I will tell you who you are."

Just for Today

Smile at a stranger.
Listen to someone's heart.
Drop a coin where a child can find it.
Learn something new, then teach it to someone.
Tell someone you're thinking of them.
Hug a loved one.
Don't hold a grudge.
Don't be afraid to say, "I'm sorry."
Look a child in the eye and tell them how great they are.
Look beyond the face of a person into their heart.
Make a promise, and keep it.
Call someone, for no other reason than to say, "Hi."
Show kindness to an animal.
Stand up for what you believe in.
Smell the rain, feel the breeze, listen to the wind.
Use all your senses to their fullest.
Cherish all your TODAYS
for they will become the yesterdays which can't be brought back.

For me, it seems my senses come alive at the beach and as such one of my favorite stories is one that is told about a young woman who like myself, loved the ocean. In fact she would go to the beach to do her writing and as the story goes, she had a habit of walking on the beach before she began her work.

One day she was walking along the shore and as she looked down the beach, she saw a human figure moving like a dancer. She smiled to herself to think of someone who would dance to the day. She began to walk faster to catch up. As she got closer, she saw that it was an old man and the old man wasn't dancing, but instead he was reaching down to the shore, picking up something and very gently throwing it into the ocean.

As she got closer, she called out, "Good morning! What are you doing?" The old man paused, looked up and replied, "Throwing starfish in the ocean."

"I guess I should have asked, why are you throwing starfish in the ocean?"

"The sun is up and the tide is going out and if I don't throw them in they'll die."

"But, old man, don't you realize that there are miles and miles of beach and starfish all along it. You can't possibly make a difference!"

The old man listened politely. Then bent down, picked up another starfish and threw it into the sea past the breaking waves and said, "It made a difference to that one."

Both the old man and the young woman had learned something. We have all been gifted with the ability to make a difference in someone's life. If we will become aware of that gift, we will gain through the strength of our visions, the power to shape the future. We must each find our starfish and if we throw our stars wisely and well, the world will be blessed.

There is something special in each and every one of us as the following work by an unknown author reiterates.

Your presence is a present to the world; you're unique and one of a kind.

Your life can be what you want it to be; take your days just one at a time.

Count your blessings, not your troubles; you'll make it through whatever comes along.

Within you are so many answers; understand, have courage, be strong.

Don't ever put limits upon yourself; you have many dreams yet to realize.

Don't leave important decisions to chance; reach for what's yours, reach for your prize.

Nothing wastes time like worrying does; the older a problem, the heavier it gets.

Don't take everything too seriously; live a life of serenity, not one of regrets.

Remember that a little love goes a long way; remember that much love goes forever.

Remember that friendship is a wise investment; life's treasures are people together.

Realize that it's never too late; do ordinary things in extraordinary ways.

Have health and hope and happiness; live life to its fullest in all of your days.

And never forget for a moment how very special you are.

Take time to dream and love what you have; take the time to wish upon a star.

The heart is a garden that always has room for the flowers of kindness that bloom.

When you reach the heart of life, you will find the beauty in all things.

The above thought is demonstrated in a story that has been circulated through every medium of communication available. It was written by Sister Helen P. Mrosia and it's titled:

All the Good Things

He was in the first third-grade class I taught at Saint Mary's School in Morris, Minnesota. All 34 of my students were dear to me, but Mark Eklund was one in a million. Very neat in appearance, he had that happy-to-be-alive attitude that made even his occasional mischievousness delightful. Mark talked incessantly. I had to remind him again and again that talking without permission was not acceptable. What impressed me so much though was his sincere response every time I had to correct him for misbehaving. "Thank you for correcting me, Sister!"

I didn't know what to make of it at first, but before long I became accustomed to hearing it many times a day. One morning my patience was growing thin when Mark talked once too often and then I made a novice-teacher mistake. I looked at him and said, "If you say one more word, I am going to tape your mouth shut!" It wasn't 10 seconds later when Chuck blurted out, "Mark is talking again." I hadn't asked any of the students to help me watch Mark, but since I had stated the punishment in front of the class, I had to act on it.

I remember the scene as if it had occurred this morning. I walked to my desk, very deliberately, opened my drawer and took out a roll of masking tape. Without saying a word, I proceeded to Mark's desk, tore off two pieces of tape and made a big X with them over his mouth. I then returned to the front of the room. As I glanced at Mark to see how he was doing he winked at me. That did it! I started laughing. The class cheered as I walked back to Mark's desk, removed the tape and shrugged my shoulders. His first words were, "Thank you for correcting me, Sister."

At the end of the year I was asked to teach junior high math. The years flew by and before I knew it Mark was in my classroom again. He was more handsome than ever and just as polite. Since he had to listen carefully to my instructions in the "new math," he did not talk as much in ninth grade as he had in the third. One Friday, things just didn't feel right. We had worked hard on a new concept all week and I sensed that the students were frowning, frustrated with themselves, and edgy with one another. I had to stop this crankiness before it got out of hand.

So I asked them to list the names of the other students in the room on two sheets of paper, leaving a space between each name. Then I told them to think of the nicest thing they could say about each of their classmates and write it down. It took the remainder of the class period to finish the assignment and as the students left the room, each one handed me the papers. Charlie smiled. Mark said, "Thank you for teaching me, Sister. Have a good weekend."

That Saturday I wrote down the name of each student on a separate sheet of paper and I listed what everyone else had said about that individual. On Monday I gave each student his or her list. Before long, the entire class was smiling. "Really?" I heard whispered. "I never knew that meant anything to anyone!" "I didn't know others liked me so much!" No one ever mentioned those papers again. I never knew if they discussed them after class or with their parents, but it didn't matter. The exercise had accomplished its purpose. The students were happy with themselves and one another again.

That group of students moved on. Several years later, after I returned from vacation, my parents met me at the airport. As we were driving home, mother asked me the usual questions about the trip, the weather, my experiences in general. There was a light lull in the conversation. Mother gave dad a sideways glance and simply said, "Dad?" My father cleared his throat as he usually did before something important. "The Eklunds called last night," he began. "Really?" I said. "I haven't heard from them in years. I wonder how Mark is." Dad responded quietly. "Mark was killed in Vietnam," he said. "The funeral is tomorrow and his parents would like it if you could attend." To this day I can still point to the exact spot on I-494 where dad told me about Mark.

I had never seen a serviceman in a military coffin before. Mark looked so handsome, so mature. All I could think at that moment was, "Mark, I would give all the masking tape in the world if only you would talk to me."

The church was packed with Mark's friends. Chuck's sister sang "The Battle Hymn of the Republic." Why did it have to rain on the day of the funeral? It was difficult enough at the graveside. The pastor said the usual prayers and the bugler played taps. One by one those who loved Mark took a last walk by the coffin. I was the last one to pass the coffin. As I stood there, one of the soldiers who had acted as pallbearer came up to me. "Were you Mark's math teacher?" he asked. I nodded as I continued to stare at the coffin. "Mark talked about you a lot," he said.

After the funeral, most of Mark's former classmates headed to Chuck's farmhouse for lunch. Mark's mother and father were there, obviously waiting for me. "We want to show you something," his father said, taking a wallet out of his pocket. "They found this on Mark when he was killed. We thought you might recognize it." Opening the billfold, he carefully removed two worn pieces of notebook paper that had obviously been taped, folded and refolded many times. I knew without looking that the papers were the ones on which I had listed all the good things each of Mark's class-mates had said about him. "Thank you so much for doing that," Mark's mother said. "As you can see, Mark treasured it."

Mark's classmates started to gather around us. Charlie smiled rather sheepishly and said, "I still have my list. It's in the top drawer of my desk at home." Chuck's wife said, "Chuck asked me to put his in our wedding album." "I have mine too," Marilyn said. "It's in my diary." Then Vicki, another classmate reached into her pocketbook, took out her wallet and showed her worn and frazzled list to the group. "I carry this with me at all times," Vicki said without batting an eyelash. "I think we all saved our lists." That's when I finally sat down and cried. I cried for Mark and for all his friends who would never see him again.

What an incredible message—the value and importance of self-esteem. Beginning today, if you love someone, tell them. Let your friends know how much they mean to you. Stay close to them for they have helped you become the person you are.

He has achieved success who has lived well, laughed often, and loved much.

The following story is titled *Something for Stevie*. Although the author is unknown the message is dynamic. It's guaranteed to move your emotions.

I try not to be biased, but I had my doubts about hiring Stevie. His placement counselor assured me that he would be a good, reliable busboy, but I had never had a mentally handicapped employee and wasn't sure I wanted one. I wasn't sure how my customers would react to Stevie. He was short, a little dumpy with the smooth facial features and thick-tongued speech of Down syndrome. I wasn't worried about most of my trucker customers because truckers don't generally care who buses tables as long as the meatloaf platter is good and the pies are homemade.

The four-wheel drivers were the ones who concerned me, the mouthy college kids traveling to school, the yuppie snobs who secretly polish their silverware with their napkins for fear of catching some dreaded "truckstop germ," and the pairs of white-shirted business men on expense accounts who think every truckstop waitress wants to be flirted with. I knew those people would be uncomfortable around Stevie so I closely watched him for the first few weeks.

I shouldn't have worried. After the first week, Stevie had my staff wrapped around his stubby little finger, and within a month my truck regulars had adopted him as their official truckstop mascot. After that, I really didn't care what the rest of the customers thought of him. He was a 21-year-old in blue jeans and Nikes, eager to laugh and eager to please, but fierce in his attention to his duties.

Every salt and pepper shaker was exactly in its place, not a bread crumb or coffee spill was visible when Stevie got done with the table. Our only problem was convincing him to wait to clean a table until after the customers were finished. He would hover in the background, shifting his weight from one foot to the other scanning the dining room until a table was empty. Then he would scurry to the empty table and carefully put the dishes and glasses onto a cart and meticulously wipe the table up with a practiced flourish of his rag.

If he thought a customer was watching, his brow would pucker with added concentration. He took pride in doing his job exactly right, and you had to love how hard he tried to please each and every person he met.

Over time we learned that he lived with his mother, a widow who was disabled after repeated surgeries for cancer. They lived on their Social Security benefits in public housing two miles from the truckstop. Their social worker, who stopped to check on Stevie every so often, admitted they had fallen between the cracks. Money was tight and what I paid him was probably the difference between them being able to live together and Stevie being sent to a group home.

That's why the restaurant was a gloomy place that morning last August, the first morning in three years that Stevie missed work. He was at the Mayo Clinic in Rochester getting a new valve or something put in his heart. His social worker said that people with Down syndrome often had heart problems at an early age so this wasn't unexpected and there was a good chance he would come through the surgery in good shape and be back at work in a few months.

A ripple of excitement ran through the staff later that morning when word came that he was out of surgery, in recovery and doing fine. Frannie, my head waitress, let out a war hoop and did a little dance in the aisle when she heard the good news. Belle Ringer, one of our regular trucker customers, stared at the sight of the 50-year-old grandmother of four doing a victory shimmy beside his table. Frannie blushed, smoothed her apron and shot Belle Ringer a withering look.

He grinned. "Okay Frannie, what was that all about?" he asked.

"We just got word that Stevie is out of surgery and going to be okay."

"I was wondering where he was. I had a new joke to tell him. What was the surgery about?"

Frannie quickly told Belle Ringer and the other two drivers sitting at his booth about Stevie's surgery, then sighed. "Yeah, I'm glad he is going to be okay," she said, "but I don't know how he and his mom are going to handle all the bills. From what I hear they're barely getting by as it is." Belle Ringer nodded thoughtfully and Frannie hurried off to wait on the rest of her tables.

Since I hadn't had time to round up a busboy to replace Stevie and really didn't want to replace him, the girls were busing their own tables that day until we decided what to do. After the morning rush, Frannie walked into my office. She had a couple of paper napkins in her hand and a funny look on her face. "What's up?" I asked.

"I didn't get that table where Belle Ringer and his friends were sitting cleared off after they left, and Pete Pony and Tony Tipper were sitting there when I got back to clean it off," she said. "This was folded and tucked under a coffee cup." She handed the napkin to me, and three $20 bills fell onto my desk when I opened it. On the outside, in big bold letters, was printed "Something for Stevie."

Pete Pony asked me what that was all about," she said, "so I told him about Stevie and his mom and everything and Pete looked at Tony and Tony looked at Pete, and they ended up giving me this." She handed me another paper napkin that had "Something for Stevie" scrawled on its outside. Two $50 bills were tucked within its folds.

Frannie looked at me with wet shiny eyes, shook her head and said simply "truckers."

That was three months ago. Today is Thanksgiving, the first day Stevie is supposed to be back at work. His placement worker said he's been counting the days until the doctor said he could work, and it didn't matter at all that it was a holiday. He called 10 times in the past week, making sure we knew he was coming, fearful that we had forgotten him or that his job was in jeopardy. I arranged to have his mother bring him to work, met them in the parking lot and invited them both to celebrate his day back.

Stevie was thinner and paler, but couldn't stop grinning as he pushed through the doors and headed for the back room where his apron and busing cart were waiting. "Hold up there, Stevie, not so fast," I said. I took him and his mother by their arms. "Work can wait for a minute. To celebrate you coming back, breakfast for you and your mother is on me."

I led them toward a large corner booth at the rear of the room. I could feel and hear the rest of the staff following behind as we marched through the dining room. Glancing over my shoulder, I saw booth after booth of grinning truckers empty and join the procession.

We stopped in front of the big table. Its surface was covered with coffee cups, saucers and dinner plates, all sitting slightly crooked on dozens of folded paper napkins.

"First thing you have to do Stevie, is clean up this mess," I said. I tried to sound stern. Stevie looked at me and then at his mother, then pulled out one of the napkins. It had "Something for Stevie" printed on the outside. As he picked it up, two $10 bills fell onto the table. Stevie stared at the money, then at all the napkins peeking from beneath the tableware, each with his name printed or scrawled on it.

I turned to his mother. "There's more than $10,000 in cash and checks on that table, all from truckers and trucking companies that heard about your problems. Happy Thanksgiving."

Well, it got real noisy about that time, with everybody hollering and shouting and there were a few tears as well. But you know what's funny? While everybody else was busy shaking hands and hugging each other, Stevie with a big, big smile on his face, was busy clearing all the cups and dishes from the table.

Best worker I ever hired.

Isn't that a great story? It really makes me feel good about life and reaffirms my belief in the natural goodness of man. I love stories like that! I love the "feel good" moments of life—the natural highs. With the help of a few of my friends (sounds like a country song!), I have come up with a list of 100 Natural Highs.

- Falling in love
- Laughing so hard your face hurts
- A hot shower
- A special glance
- Getting mail
- Walking barefoot in the sand
- Taking a drive on a pretty road
- Hearing your favorite song on the radio
- Lying in bed listening to the rain outside
- Hot towels out of the dryer
- Singing cheesy songs with your friends
- Walking out of your last final
- Finding the sweater you want is on sale for half price
- A chocolate milkshake
- A movie that makes you believe in love again
- A long distance phone call
- Getting invited to a dance
- Taking off high heels
- A bubble bath
- Giggling
- Falling in love
- Eating out with friends
- A good conversation
- Catching a snowflake on your tongue
- A care package
- The beach
- Making the winning score
- Finding $20 in your coat from last winter
- Laughing at yourself
- Midnight phone calls that last for hours
- Shopping trips with friends
- Running through sprinklers
- Laughing for absolutely no reason at all
- Hearing a song that reminds you of someone you love
- Having someone tell you that you're beautiful
- Knowing someone really understands
- Laughing at an inside joke
- Friends
- Falling in love for the first time
- Slumber parties
- Falling in love

- The weather matching your mood
- A surprise gift from a friend
- Accidentally overhearing someone saying something nice about you
- Waking up and realizing that you still have a few hours of sleep left
- Your first kiss
- Being part of a team
- Making new friends or spending time with old ones
- Seeing a shooting star
- Playing with a puppy
- Late night talks with your best friend that keep you from sleeping
- Having someone play with your hair
- Sweet dreams
- Looking into the eyes of the one you love
- Hot chocolate
- Road trips with friends
- Swinging on swings
- Watching a candle burn
- Watching a good movie cuddled up on the couch with someone you love
- Wrapping presents under the Christmas tree while eating cookies and drinking eggnog
- Falling in love
- Song lyrics printed inside your new CD so you can sing along without feeling stupid
- Going to a really good concert
- Getting butterflies in your stomach every time you see that one person
- Making eye contact with a cute stranger
- Winning a really competitive game
- Making chocolate chip cookies
- Saying "I love you"
- Spending time with close friends
- A porch swing
- Running through the fountains with your friends
- Riding a bike downhill
- The feeling after running a few miles
- Dressing up and knowing you look good
- The feeling you get the first time you step on a stage
- Sitting outside looking at the stars
- Seeing smiles and hearing laughter from your friends
- Holding hands with someone you care about

- A really steamy romance novel to read on a rainy day
- Running into an old friend and realizing that some things (good and bad) never change
- Falling in love
- Discovering that love is unconditional and stronger than time
- Riding the best roller coasters over and over
- Hugging the person you love
- Watching the expression on someone's face as they open a much-desired present from you
- Kisses on your forehead from the first and only boy you have ever loved
- Staying home from work on your birthday
- Watching the sunrise
- Getting out of bed every morning and thanking God for another beautiful day, even when the weather is nasty
- A great idea
- Writing something you know is good
- Listening to the sound of waves crashing on the beach
- Watching a beautiful sunset
- Holding someone you love in front of a fireplace
- Playing with a kitten
- Having someone to share your dreams with
- Wearing your boyfriend's shirt that still smells like his cologne
- Knowing that someone you love, loves you back
- A happy thought
- Falling in love

Listening Shows You Care V

A friend is someone who knows the song in your heart and sings it back to you when you have forgotten how it goes.

The little child whispered, "God, speak to me." And the meadow lark sang but the child did not hear.

So the child yelled, "God, speak to me!" And the thunder rolled across the sky but the child did not listen.

The child looked around and said, "God, let me see you." And a star shone brightly but the child did not notice.

And the child shouted, "God, show me a miracle!" And a life was born but the child did not know. So the child cried out in despair, "Touch me God and let me know you are here!"

Where upon God reached down and touched the child, but the child brushed the butterfly away and walked off unknowingly.

Take time to listen. Oftentimes the things we seek are right under our noses. Don't miss out on your blessing because it isn't packaged the way you expect.

Indeed, how many times do we miss God's blessings because they are not packaged as we expect?

A young man was getting ready to graduate from college. For many months he had admired a beautiful sports car in a dealer's showroom and knowing his father could well afford it, he told him that was all he wanted. As graduation day approached, the young man awaited signs that his father had purchased the car. Finally on the morning of his graduation, his father called him into his private study. His father told him how proud he was to have such a fine son and told him how much he loved him. He handed his son a beautifully wrapped gift box. Curious and somewhat disappointed, the young man opened the box and found a lovely, leather-bound Bible with his name embossed in gold.

Angry, he raised his voice to his father and said, "With all your money you give me a Bible?" and stormed out of the house. Many years passed and the young man was very successful in business. He had a beautiful house and wonderful family, but realized his father was very old and perhaps he should go see him. He had not seen him since that graduation day.

Before he could make arrangements, he received a telegram telling him his father had passed away and willed all of his possessions to his son. He needed to come home immediately and take care of things. When he arrived at his father's house, sudden sadness and regret filled his heart. He began to search through his father's important papers and saw the still new Bible, just as he had left it years before.

With tears, he opened the Bible and began to turn the pages. His father had carefully underlined a verse, Matthew 7:11, "And if ye, being evil, know how to give good gifts to your children, how much more shall your Heavenly Father which is in heaven give to those who ask Him?"

As he read those words, a car key dropped from the back of the Bible. It had a tag with the dealer's name, the same dealer who had the sports car he had desired. On the tag was the date of his graduation, and the words PAID IN FULL.

What an incredible message! You might be thinking right now as I'm sure the son was thinking, "If only I had known." And at other times we might hear someone say, "If only I had known then what I know now, what a difference it would have made!" I ask you, "Would it? Would it have really made a difference?" If so, you will enjoy the following list of things learned from a long life.

Age 7: I've learned that you can't hide broccoli in a glass of milk.

Age 8: I've learned that I like my teacher because she cried when we sang "Silent Night."

Age 9: I've learned that when I wave to people in the country, they stop what they are doing and wave back.

Age 12: I've learned that if you want to cheer yourself up, you should try cheering someone else up.

Age 13: I've learned that just when I get my room the way I like it, Mom makes me clean it up.

Age 15: I've learned that although it's hard to admit it, I'm secretly glad my parents are strict with me.

Age 24: I've learned that silent company is often more healing than words of advice.

Age 26: I've learned that brushing my child's hair is one of life's greatest pleasures.

Age 29: I've learned that wherever I go, the world's worst drivers have followed me there.

Age 39: I've learned that if someone says something unkind about me, I must live so that no one will believe it.

Age 41: I've learned that there are people who love you dearly but just don't know how to show it.

Age 44: I've learned that you can make someone's day by simply sending them a little card.

Age 46: I've learned that the greater the person's sense of guilt, the greater his need to cast blame on others.

Age 47: I've learned that children and grandparents are natural allies.

Age 49: I've learned that singing "Amazing Grace" can lift my spirits for hours.

Age 50: I've learned that motel mattresses are better on the side away from the phone.

Age 52: I've learned that you can tell a lot about a man by the way he handles these three things: a rainy day, lost luggage and tangled Christmas tree lights.

Age 53: I've learned that regardless of your relationship with your parents, you miss them terribly after they die.

Age 58: I've learned that making a living is not the same thing as making a life.

Age 61: I've learned that if you want to do something positive for your children, try to improve your marriage.

Age 62: I've learned that life sometimes gives you a second chance.

Age 64: I've learned that you shouldn't go through life with a catcher's mitt on both hands. You need to be able to throw something back.

Age 65: I've learned that if you pursue happiness, it will elude you. But if you focus on your family, the needs of others, your work, meeting new people and doing the very best you can, happiness will find you.

Age 66: I've learned that whenever I decide something with kindness, I usually make the right decision.

Age 72: I've learned that everyone can use a prayer.

Age 73: I've learned that it pays to believe in miracles. And to tell the truth, I've seen several.

Age 82: I've learned that even when I have pains, I don't have to be one.

Age 85: I've learned that every day you should reach out and touch someone. People love that human touch—holding hands, a warm hug, or just a friendly pat on the back. And I've learned that sometimes when we are younger, we are so busy we fail to hear the music until it is over.

Have you ever watched kids on a merry-go-round or listened to the rain? Have you ever followed a butterfly's erratic flight or gazed at the sun into the fading night?

You better slow down; don't dance so fast. Time is short; the music won't last.

Do you run through each day on the fly and when you ask, "How are you?" do you hear the reply? When the day is done, do you lie in your bed with the next hundred chores running through your head?

You'd better slow down; don't dance so fast. Time is short; the music won't last.

Have you ever told your child, "We'll do it tomorrow," and in your haste not seen his sorrow? Have you ever lost touch, let a good friendship die because you never had time to call and say, "Hi"?

You'd better slow down; don't dance so fast. Time is short; the music won't last.

When you run so fast to get somewhere, you miss half the fun of getting there. When you worry and hurry through your day, it's like an unopened gift thrown away.

Life is not a race. Do take it slower. Hear the music before it is over.

There will be many people who will walk in and out of your life, but only true friends will live in your heart. And now for a poem by an unknown author to get you thinking.

How Many Friends Have You?

The old man turned to me and asked, "How many friends have you?"
Why 10 or 20 friends have I and named off just a few.
He rose quite slowly with effort and sadly shook his head.
A lucky child are you to have so many friends he said.
But think of what you are saying; there is so much you do not know.
A friend is not someone to whom you just say "hello."
A friend's a tender shoulder on which to softly cry.
A well to pour your troubles down and raise your spirits high.
A friend's a hand to pull you up from darkness and despair.
When all your other "so called" friends have helped to put you there.
A true friend is an ally who can't be moved or bought.
A voice to keep your name alive when others have forgot.
But most of all, a friend's a heart; a strong and sturdy wall.
For from the hearts of friends, there comes the greatest love of all!
So think of what I've spoken for every word is true.
And answer once again my child, "How many friends have you?"
And then he stood and faced me, awaiting my reply.
Soft and sad I answered, "If lucky...one have I."

As we go through life, our idea of what a good friend is changes. For instance, in kindergarten, your idea of a good friend was the person who let you have the red crayon when all that was left was the ugly black one. Then in first grade, your idea of a good friend was the person who went to the bathroom with you and held your hand as you walked through the scary halls. In second grade, your idea of a good friend was the person who helped you stand up to the class bully.

The person who shared lunch with you when you forgot yours on the bus was your idea of a good friend in third grade. In fourth grade your idea of a good friend was the person who was willing to switch square dance partners in gym class so you wouldn't have to be stuck do-si-doing with Nasty Nick or Smelly Susan. The person who saved a seat for you on the back of the bus was your idea of a good friend in fifth grade.

Your idea of a good friend in sixth grade was the person who went up to Nasty Nick or Smelly Susan, your new crush, and asked them to dance with you so that if they said no you wouldn't be embarrassed. The person who let you copy the social studies homework that you hadn't done from the night before was your idea of a good friend in seventh grade. In eighth grade your idea of a good friend was the person who helped you pack up your stuffed animals and old baseball cards so that your room would be a "high schooler's" room, but didn't laugh at you when you finished and broke out in tears.

In ninth grade your idea of a good friend was the person who went with you to that "cool" party thrown by a senior so you wouldn't wind up being the only freshman there. The person who changed their schedule so you would have someone to sit with at lunch was your idea of a good friend in tenth grade. In eleventh grade your idea of a good friend was the person who gave you rides in their new car, convinced your parents that you shouldn't be grounded, consoled you when you broke up with Nick or Susan and found you a date to the prom. Your idea of a good friend in twelfth grade was the person who helped you pick out a college, assured you that you would get into that college and helped you deal with your parents who were having a hard time adjusting to the idea of letting go.

At graduation your idea of a good friend was the person who was crying on the inside but managed the biggest smile one could give as they congratulated you. The summer after twelfth grade your idea of a good friend was the person who helped you clean up the bottles from that party, helped you sneak out of the house when you just couldn't deal with your parents, assured you that now that you and Nick, or you and Susan were back together you could make it through anything, helped you pack for college and silently hugged you as you looked through blurry eyes at 18 years of memories you were leaving behind. And finally on those last days of childhood, went out of their way to come over and send you off with a hug, a lot of memories, reassurance that you would make it in college as well as you had the past 18 years and most importantly, sent you off to college knowing you were loved.

Now your idea of a good friend is still the person who gives you the better of the two choices, holds your hand when you're scared, helps you fight off those who try to take advantage of you, thinks of you at times when you are not there, reminds you of what you have forgotten, helps you put the past behind you but understands when you need to hold on to it a little longer, stays with you so that you have confidence, goes out of their way to make time for you, helps you clear up your mistakes, helps you deal with pressure from others, smiles for you when they are sad, helps you become a better person and most importantly loves you!

What a blessing good friends are! Speaking of love, here is a poem by an unknown author with an incredible message of love. It's titled:

Not Yet

Sometimes I ask the question, "My Lord, is this your will?"
It's then I hear you answer me, "My Precious Child, be still."
Sometimes I feel frustrated, because I think I know what's best.
It's then I hear you say to me, "My Busy Child, just rest."
Sometimes I feel so lonely and I think I'd like a mate.
Your still small voice gets oh so clear and says, "My Child, please wait."
I know the plans I have for you, the wondrous things you'll see;
If you can just be patient, Child, and put your trust in me.
I've plans to draw you closer. I've plans to help you grow.
There's much I do you cannot see and much you do not know.
But know this Child, I love you. You are Precious unto Me.
Before I formed you in the womb, I planned your destiny.
I've something very special I hope for you to learn.
The gifts I wish to give to you are gifts you cannot earn.
They come without a price tag, but not without a cost;
At Calvary I gave my Son so you would not be lost.
Rest Child and do not weary of doing what is good.
I promise I'll come back for you just like I said I would.
Your name is written on my palm, I never could forget;
Therefore do not be discouraged when my answer is..."Not Yet."

Good friends...what precious gifts they are in our life! Several years back a friend of mine shared a list of gifts with me and now I'd like to share them with you.

First and foremost is the gift of listening. Try giving this to someone in need. You must really listen—no interrupting, no daydreaming, no planning your response. Just listen.

Next is the gift of signs of affection. Be generous with your hugs, kisses and gentle squeezes of the hand for these tiny actions demonstrate the love inside of you.

Third is the gift of a note. It can be as simple as "I Love You" or as creative as a sonnet placed where it will surprise your loved one.

The gift of laughter is easily shared by clipping a cartoon or a clever article. Your gift will say, "I love to laugh with you."

Fifth is the gift of a compliment. Sharing a simple "You look good in blue" or "Good supper" can be of the greatest value to those who may feel they are being taken for granted.

Another gift is the gift of a favor. Little things that can mean so much, like helping with the dishes or running an errand.

Seventh is the gift of leaving someone alone. There are times in our lives when we want nothing better than to be left alone. Become more sensitive to those times and give solitude.

Next is the gift of a cheerful disposition. Try to be cheerful around those you love.

Ninth is the gift of a game. Offer to play your loved one's favorite game; even if you lose, you'll be a winner.

And last but not least, the gift of prayer. Pray for your loved ones and let them know you pray for them.

Speaking of gifts, there's an interesting story that is told about a wealthy family man who took his son on a trip to the country so he could have his son see how poor country people were.

They stayed one day and one night in a very humble farm house. At the end of the trip and back home, the father asked the son some questions. He began with, "What did you think of the trip?" To this the son replied, "Very nice dad." Next the father asked his son, "Did you notice how poor they were?" "Yes," he replied to which the father then asked, "What did you learn?"

The son looked at his father and said, "I learned that we have one dog in the house and they have four. We have a fountain in the garden and they have a stream that has no end. We have imported lamps in the garden and they have the stars. Our garden goes to the edge of our property while they have an entire horizon as their backyard."

At the end of the son's reply the father was speechless and his son added, "Thank you dad for showing me how poor we really are."

There are stories that have been passed down to me from friends of mine who do not know the source of the story but from them we can learn some incredible life lessons. Here are several such lessons, each from a different unknown source.

Lesson 1: The Most Important Question

During my second month of night school, our professor gave us a pop quiz. I was a conscientious student and had breezed through the questions, until I read the last one: "What is the first name of the woman who cleans the school?" Obviously, this was some kind of joke. I had seen the cleaning woman several times. She was tall, dark-haired and in her 50s, but how would I know her name? I handed in my paper, leaving the last question blank.

Before class ended, one student asked if the last question would count toward our quiz grade. "Absolutely," said the professor. "In your lives, in your careers, you will meet many people. All are significant. They deserve your attention and care, even if all you do is smile and say "Hello."

I've never forgotten that lesson. I also learned her name was Dorothy.

Lesson 2: Pickup in the Rain

One night at 11:30 p.m., an older African American woman was standing on the side of an Alabama highway trying to endure a lashing rainstorm. Her car had broken down and she desperately needed a ride. Soaking wet, she decided to flag down the next car. A young white man stopped to help her; generally unheard of in those conflict-filled 1960s.

The man took her to safety, helped her get assistance and put her into a taxi cab. She seemed to be in a big hurry! She wrote down his address, thanked him and drove away.

Seven days went by and a knock came on the man's door. To his surprise, a giant color TV was delivered to his house. A special note was attached. It read: "Thank you so much for assisting me on the highway the other night. The rain drenched not only my clothes but my spirits. Then you came along. Because of you, I was able to make it to my dying husband's bedside just before he passed away. God bless you for helping me and unselfishly serving others." It was signed, "Sincerely, Mrs. Nat King Cole."

Lesson 3: Always Remember Those Who Serve

In the days when an ice cream sundae cost much less, a 10-year-old boy entered a hotel coffee shop and sat at a table. A waitress put a glass of water in front of him. "How much is an ice cream sundae?" "Fifty cents," replied the waitress. The little boy pulled his hand out of his pocket and studied a number of coins in it. "How much is a dish of plain ice cream?"

he inquired. Some people were now waiting for a table and the waitress was a bit impatient. "Thirty-five cents," she said brusquely. The little boy again counted the coins. "I'll have the plain ice cream," he said.

The waitress brought the ice cream, put the bill on the table and walked away. The boy finished the ice cream, paid the cashier and departed.

When the waitress came back, she began wiping down the table and then swallowed hard at what she saw. There, placed neatly beside the empty dish was 15 cents, her tip.

Lesson 4: Giving Blood

Many years ago when I worked as a volunteer at Stanford Hospital, I got to know a little girl named Liz who was suffering from a rare and serious disease. Her only chance of recovery appeared to be a blood transfusion from her five-year-old brother, who had miraculously survived the same disease and had developed the antibodies needed to combat the illness. The doctor explained the situation to her little brother and asked the boy if he would be willing to give his blood to his sister. I saw him hesitate for only a moment before taking a deep breath and saying, "Yes, I'll do it if it will save Liz."

As the transfusion progressed, he lay in bed next to his sister and smiled as we all did, seeing the color returning to her cheeks. Then his face grew pale and his smile faded. He looked up at the doctor and asked with a trembling voice, "Will I start to die right away?" Being young, the boy had misunderstood the doctor; he thought he was going to have to give his sister all of his blood.

The fifth lesson deals with understanding and forgiveness. It is a story that most parents I am sure can relate to.

As I sat perched in the second-floor window of our brick schoolhouse that afternoon, my heart began to sink further with each passing car. This was a day I'd looked forward to for weeks. Miss Pace's fourth-grade, end-of-the-year party. Miss Pace had kept a running countdown on the blackboard all week and our class of nine-year-olds had bordered on insurrection by the time the much-anticipated "Friday party" had arrived.

I had happily volunteered my mother when Miss Pace requested cookie volunteers. Mom's chocolate chips reigned supreme on our block and I knew they'd be a hit with my classmates. But two o'clock passed and there was no sign of her. Most of the other mothers had already come and gone, dropping off their offerings of punch and crackers, chips, cupcakes and brownies. My mother was missing in action.

"Don't worry Robbie, she'll be along soon," Miss Pace said as I gazed forlornly down at the street. I looked at the wall clock just in time to see its black minute hand shift to half-past.

Around me, the noisy party raged on, but I wouldn't budge from my window watch post. Miss Pace did her best to coax me away, but I stayed put, holding out hope that the familiar family car would round the corner, carrying my rightfully embarrassed mother with a tin of her famous cookies tucked under her arm.

The three o'clock bell soon jolted me from my thoughts and I dejectedly grabbed my book bag from my desk and shuffled out the door for home.

On the four-block walk to our house, I plotted my revenge. I would slam the front door upon entering, refuse to return her hug when she rushed over to me and vow never to speak to her again.

The house was empty when I arrived and I looked for a note on the refrigerator that might explain my mother's absence, but found none. My chin quivered with a mixture of heartbreak and rage. For the first time in my life, my mother had let me down.

I was lying face-down on my bed upstairs when I heard her come through the front door. "Robbie," she called out a bit urgently. "Where are you?"

I could hear her darting frantically from room to room, wondering where I could be. I remained silent. In a moment she mounted the steps; the sounds of her footsteps quickening as she ascended the staircase.

When she entered my room and sat beside me on my bed, I didn't move but instead stared blankly into my pillow refusing to acknowledge her presence.

"I'm so sorry honey," she said. "I just forgot. I got busy and forgot, plain and simple." I still didn't move. "Don't forgive her," I told myself. "She humiliated you. She forgot you. Make her pay."

Then my mother did something completely unexpected. She began to laugh. I could feel her shudder as the laughter shook her. It began quietly at first and then increased in its velocity and volume.

I was incredulous. How could she laugh at a time like this? I rolled over and faced her, ready to let her see the rage and disappointment in my eyes.

But my mother wasn't laughing at all. She was crying. "I'm so sorry," she sobbed softly. "I let you down. I let my little boy down."

She sat down on the bed and began to weep like a little girl. I was dumbstruck. I had never seen my mother cry. To my understanding, mothers weren't supposed to. I wondered if this was how I looked to her when I cried.

I desperately tried to recall her own soothing words from times past when I'd skinned knees or stubbed toes, times when she knew just the right thing to say. But in that moment of tearful plight, words of profundity abandoned me like a worn-out shoe.

"It's okay, Mom," I stammered as I reached out and gently stroked her hair. "We didn't even need those cookies. There was plenty of stuff to eat. Don't cry. It's all right. Really."

My words, as inadequate as they sounded to me, prompted my mother to sit up. She wiped her eyes and a slight smile began to crease her tear-stained cheeks. I smiled back awkwardly and she pulled me to her.

We didn't say another word. We just held each other in a long, silent embrace. When we came to the point where I would usually pull away, I decided that this time, I could hold on, perhaps, just a little bit longer.

Sometimes listening is more than hearing, which brings us to the end of this chapter. At this point I would like to share what I consider some of the highlights of this book. Following are 45 suggestions to help you have the incredible life you deserve.

1. Give people more than they expect and do it cheerfully.
2. Memorize your favorite poem.
3. Don't believe all you hear, spend all you have or sleep all you want.
4. When you say "I love you," mean it.
5. When you say "I'm sorry," look the person in the eye.
6. Be engaged at least six months before you get married.
7. Believe in love at first sight.
8. Never laugh at anyone's dreams. People who don't have dreams don't have much.
9. Love deeply and passionately. You might get hurt but it's the only way to live life completely.
10. In disagreements, fight fairly. No name calling.
11. Don't judge people by their relatives.
12. Talk slowly but think quickly.
13. When someone asks you a question you don't want to answer, smile and ask, "Why do you want to know?"
14. Remember that real love and great achievements involve great risk.

15. Ask questions.
16. Say "bless you" when you hear someone sneeze.
17. When you lose, don't lose the lesson.
18. Remember the three Rs: Respect for self, Respect for others, and Responsibility for all your actions.
19. Don't let a little dispute injure a great friendship.
20. When you realize you've made a mistake, take immediate steps to correct it.
21. Smile when you pick up the phone. The caller will hear it in your voice.
22. Marry a man/woman you love to talk to. As you get older, their conversational skills will be as important as any other.
23. Spend time alone.
24. Open your arms to change, but don't let go of your values.
25. Remember that silence is sometimes the best answer.
26. Read more books and watch less TV.
27. Live a good, honorable life. Then when you get older and think back, you'll get to enjoy it a second time.
28. Trust in God, but lock your car.
29. A loving atmosphere in your home is so important. Do all you can to create a tranquil, harmonious home.
30. In disagreements with loved ones, deal with the current situation.
31. Read between the lines.
32. Share your knowledge. It's a way to achieve immortality.
33. Be gentle with the earth.
34. Pray. There's immeasurable power in it.
35. Never interrupt when you are being flattered.
36. Mind your own business.
37. Don't trust a man/woman who doesn't close his/her eyes when you kiss.
38. Once a year, go someplace you've never been before.
39. If you make a lot of money, put it to use helping others while you are living. That is wealth's greatest satisfaction.
40. Remember that not getting what you want is sometimes a stroke of luck.
41. Learn the rules and then break some.
42. Remember that the best relationship is one where your love of each other is greater than your need for each other.
43. Judge your success by what you had to give up to get it.
44. Remember that your character is your destiny.
45. Approach love and cooking with reckless abandon.

Learning to Laugh

Laughter is the shortest distance between two people.

There's a quote I have hanging on the bulletin board at my office, stuck in the flap of my appointment calendar, in a pocket of my purse and in my wallet. It's a simple quote with an incredible message. Quite simply it says:

People will forget what you said,
People will forget what you did,
But people will never forget how you made them feel.

LIVE WELL. LAUGH OFTEN. LOVE MUCH.

Find time in each day to see the beauty and love in the world around you. Forget what happened yesterday; it's over. Likewise, don't anticipate what might happen in the future, for tomorrow might never get here. Create your own space within your house where you will not be bothered by your obligations and use this space daily, even if only for 20 minutes.

In the midst of controversy, concentrate only on your own feelings and reactions, not on those around you. Accept that you can only speak for your own self and that you add extreme stress and disappointment to your own life when your expectations about others become a major focus. Live by inner-focus instead of outer-focus. Live by actions rather than reactions. Life is like a mirage in the desert. What you see and hear is not really happening. What is happening is only your interpretation of what you see and hear.

Use others as mirrors of your self. What one sees in others is also a personal interpretation, usually telling us more about our own selves. Throw a tantrum every now and then. It feels good to defend your own feelings and your own ideas. Keep away from those who want to change you. You can do without the disapproval of others. Those who constantly disapprove are not living their own lives but trying to live yours. By the same token, do not live your own life trying to change others.

Create chaos out of order occasionally; it's fun. Life is fun, life is beautiful, life is a mystery; accept it without trying to explain it. Read history; it keeps today's news in perspective.

Find time in each day to see the beauty and love in the world around you. Realize that each person has limitless abilities, but each of us is different in our own way. What you may feel you lack in one regard may be more than compensated for in another. What you feel you lack in the present may become one of your strengths in the future. May you see your future as one filled with promise and possibility. Learn to view everything as a worthwhile experience. May you find enough inner strength to determine your own worth by yourself and not be dependent on another's judgment of your accomplishments. May you always feel loved.

A popular artist today is best known for his nostalgic renditions of friendship and love. Kim Anderson uses pictures of children dressed in Sunday best. One such picture was a gift from a friend of mine one Valentine's Day. Three small pictures are framed with a caption between them. The first picture is of three little girls at a soda fountain; the next picture has two little girls waiting on the steps and the third picture shows the little girls sharing a secret. The caption reads: "Of all the blessings that time and life bestow, there is none so precious as a friend."

How true! And how easily we sometimes forget. A friend sent me a poem by an unknown author titled:

Why God Made Little Girls

God made the world with its towering trees
Majestic mountains and restless seas.
Then paused and said,
"It needs one more thing
Someone to laugh and dance and sing.
To walk in the woods and gather flowers
To commune with nature in quiet hours."

So God made little girls
With laughing eyes and bouncing curls
With joyful hearts and infectious smiles
Enchanting ways and feminine wiles,
And when he'd completed the task he'd begun,
He was pleased and proud of the job he'd done
For the world when seen through a little girl's eyes
Greatly resembles Paradise.

To finish the moment, to find the journey's end in every step of the road, to live the greatest number of good hours, is wisdom.

Ralph Waldo Emerson

What a wonderful tribute to little girls and certainly reminds me of a Kim Anderson print. And now for:

Why God Made Little Boys

God made a world out of his dreams,
Of wondrous mountains, oceans and streams,
Prairies and plains and wooded land,
Then paused and thought,
"I need someone to stand on top of the mountains
To conquer the seas, explore the plains and
Climb the trees, someone to start small and grow,
Sturdy, strong like a tree and so..."

He created boys, full of spirit and fun,
To explore and conquer, to romp and run
With dirty faces, banged up chins
With courageous hearts and boyish grins.
When He had completed the task He'd begun
He surely said, "That's a job well done."

Speaking of the blessings of time and life, I have a picture that was taken of my dad and my grandson shortly before my dad passed away. It was taken at a McDonald's playhouse and is a beautiful example of time with the old man nearing the end of his life and the little boy just beginning his. And so goes the cycle of life. In the picture the two are sharing more than a meal; they are sharing time, enjoying each other's company. There's a story that is told about Grandpa's keys and it reminds me of what dad and Cody shared. I'm not sure whose story it is. It could be yours.

When I was a young boy about 10 years old I used to visit my Grandpa and Grandma. I did not realize at the time but my grandparents were baby-sitting me while my parents had things to do and I might get in the way. I sure didn't care if I stayed with Grandma and Grandpa because the day was always filled with happy times.

Grandma would fix my favorite dinner along with my favorite desserts. Grandpa would sit and tell stories about when he was young. He told me stories about Rover, his pet dog. He would tell me stories about when he was in the army. He talked about the good times, his dreams, his friendships and the things he liked most. He made up stories that stirred my very soul.

I would close my eyes and sail the pirate ships. I would fight the fire-breathing dragons. I would travel the stars in spaceships and experience adventures under the sea. Most of all I remember what looked like a hundred keys that Grandpa had hanging on a nail at the back door. Grandpa had fashioned a piece of wire into a large loop with a clever hook that held the loop together much like a safety pin. All the keys were hanging from this wire loop.

Grandpa would put a towel on the kitchen table and I would take all the keys off the wire and line them up on the towel. Grandpa would caution me not to lose any of the keys. I would organize all the keys into groups of similar-looking keys and keys of the same color. He had some long black keys that looked like a nail with a round end and long black teeth on the other end. He would pick up each key and gently rub it between his finger and thumb and tell me about it.

"This one is for the front door of the house. This is the one to the house where your mom and dad lived before you were born. This is the key to my mother's house, your great-grandmother, before it burned down 25 years ago. This is my skeleton key," he would say with a smile. I loved my Grandpa very much, but I was not about to ask any questions about his skeleton key.

Grandpa also had some brass keys, which he studied with his keen eyes. "This is the key to my old Ford that wore out many years ago. This is the key to the Oldsmobile that I drive now and this is the key to the trunk of my car. This is the key to the car that Grandma used to drive, and this is the key to the garage." Grandpa never does lock the garage though.

Grandpa lovingly studied more keys. "This is the key to the storage shed. Sometimes on Sunday I go over to the church to start the furnace so this is the key to the church." Then Grandpa picked up a strange-looking key and smiled. "This is a skate key. This is the key to my bicycle lock." Grandpa had not had a bicycle in over 30 years and who knows when he used to skate. Then Grandpa picked up the strangest looking key I had ever seen. "This is not a key at all," he laughed. "It is a wrench for tightening up my bicycle spokes."

"This is the key to the office building where I used to work, this is the key to the front door for the office and this little key fits the file cabinet there." Grandpa retired 15 years ago. Grandpa then picked up about 20 keys from the table and explained, "These keys are LFL keys." Then he smiled and explained LFL meant long-forgotten locks.

Grandpa also had another ring of keys that were hung very high on the back door frame. These keys were much larger, the ring was gold in color and was welded so it could not be opened to remove the keys. Grandpa explained that these keys were hung on the highest point on the door because they were the most important keys of all and were not to be played with because they were so valuable. He said when I got older he was going to give me those special keys.

Each key was about five inches long and had words printed on it. Grandpa told me that the special keys were the keys to everything important. These are the keys of life and the keys to heaven. The wording on each key must be studied, lived and its message imprinted in your brain and branded into your soul. Grandpa lived up to his promise. On my 18th birthday I went to visit Grandma and Grandpa. He tenderly handed the keys to me. When I studied the keys I realized what my Grandpa meant when he spoke of the keys.

The first key was gold in color and the most important of all the keys. On one side it said *LOVE* and on the other side it said, "Love of God, fellow man, friends, family and children. Love of country, love of God's creations and love of God's unfortunate souls."

The second key and all of the other keys were silver. On one side it said *FORGIVE*. On the other side it said, "Forgive your enemy, forgive those who do you harm, forgive those who say and do unkind things to you or about you."

The third key said *PATIENCE*. On the reverse side it said, "Patience of people, traffic, long lines, those who fail to show patience and patience toward children, old people and the handicapped.

The fourth key said *UNDERSTANDING*. Try to see the other side of the issue.

The fifth key said *HAPPINESS*. Be happy even in adversity. Remember every cloud has a silver lining and as the cloud passes, the sun will shine again.

The sixth key said *THANKFUL*. Be thankful for all you have and do not be saddened by the things you do not have.

The seventh key said *INDUSTRIOUS*. Remember if a job is worth doing, it is worth doing right and a honest day's work for an honest day's pay.

The eighth key said *CLEANLINESS*. Keep your body and your mind clean. Cleanliness is next to Godliness.

The ninth key said *HONESTY*. Be truthful at all times and remember some of the worst lies are shrouded in silence.

The tenth key said *EDUCATION*. Learn to be all you can be. Do not let your mind go to waste.

What a wonderful legacy to pass on to your grandchildren. Indeed, it would do us all well to realize the value of time and life and love and keep all of them in their proper perspectives.

Perhaps it would help if you were to imagine there is a bank that credits your account each morning with $86,400. It carries over no balance from day to day. Every evening it deletes whatever part of the balance you failed to use during the day. What would you do? Draw out every cent, of course!

Each of us has such a bank. Its name is *time*. Every morning, it credits you with 86,400 seconds. Every night it writes off, as lost, whatever of this you have failed to invest to good purpose. It carries over no balance. It allows no overdraft. Each day it opens a new account for you. Each night it burns the remains of the day. If you fail to use the day's deposits, the loss is yours. There is no going back. There is no drawing against the "tomorrow." You must live in the present on today's deposits. Invest it so as to get from it the utmost in health, happiness and success! The clock is running. Make the most of today.

To realize the value of *one year*, ask a student who failed a grade.

To realize the value of *one month*, ask a mother who gave birth to a premature baby.

To realize the value of *one week*, ask the editor of a weekly newspaper.

To realize the value of *one hour*, ask the lovers who are waiting to meet.

To realize the value of *one second*, ask a person who just avoided an accident.

To realize the value of *one millisecond*, ask the person who won a silver medal in the Olympics.

Treasure every moment that you have and treasure it more because you shared it with someone special, special enough to spend your time. And remember that time waits for no one.

Yesterday is history. Tomorrow is a mystery. Today is a gift...that's why it's called the present!

If you're like me you've postponed things, thinking that you would have more time at a later date. In fact, as I mentioned in Chapter IV, there was one such day not so long ago and had it not been for an inner voice, I would have missed my final opportunity to see my dad before he passed away. I was fortunate. I listened to my inner voice, my guardian angel if you will, and as such I was able to hug dad and tell him I loved him. The girl in the following story sent to me by a friend of mine was not as fortunate.

The hospital was unusually quiet that bleak January evening, quiet and still like the air before a storm. I stood in the nurse's station on the seventh floor and glanced at the clock. It was nine o'clock. I threw a stethoscope around my neck and headed for room 712, last room on the hall. Room 712 had a new patient, Mr. Williams. A man all alone. A man strangely silent about his family.

As I entered the room, Mr. Williams looked up eagerly, but dropped his eyes when he saw it was only me, his nurse. I pressed the stethoscope over his chest and listened. Strong, slow, even beating. Just what I wanted to hear. There seemed little indication he had suffered a slight heart attack a few hours earlier. He looked up from his starched white bed. "Nurse, would you..." He hesitated, tears filling his eyes. Once before he had started to ask me a question, but changed his mind. I touched his hand, waiting.

He brushed away a tear. "Would you call my daughter? Tell her I've had a heart attack. A slight one. You see, I live alone and she is the only family I have." His respiration suddenly speeded up. I turned his nasal oxygen up to eight liters a minute.

"Of course I'll call her," I said, studying his face. He gripped the sheets and pulled himself forward, his face tense with urgency. "Will you call her right away, as soon as you can?" He was breathing fast, too fast. "I'll call her the very first thing," I said, patting his shoulder.

I flipped off the light. He closed his eyes, such young blue eyes in his 50-year-old face. Room 712 was dark except for a faint night-light under the sink. Oxygen gurgled in the green tubes above his bed. Reluctant to leave, I moved through the shadowy silence to the window. The panes were cold. Below a foggy mist curled through the hospital parking lot. "Nurse," he called, "could you get me a pencil and paper?" I dug a scrap of yellow paper and a pen from my pocket and set it on the bedside table.

I walked back to the nurse's station and sat in a squeaky swivel chair by the phone. Mr. William's daughter was listed on his chart as the next of kin. I got her number from information and dialed. Her soft voice answered. "Janie, this is Sue Kidd, a registered nurse at the hospital. I'm calling about your father. He was admitted tonight with a slight heart attack and..." "No!" she screamed into the phone, startling me. "He's not dying, is he?" "His condition is stable at the moment," I said, trying hard to sound convincing. Silence. I bit my lip. "You must not let him die!" she said. Her voice was so utterly compelling that my hand trembled on the phone. "He is getting the very best care." "But you don't understand," she pleaded. "My daddy and I haven't spoken since we fought on my 21st birthday over my boyfriend. I ran out of the house. I haven't been back. All these months I've wanted to go to him for forgiveness. The last thing I said to him was, 'I hate you'."

Her voice cracked and I heard her heave great agonizing sobs. I sat, listening, tears burning my eyes. A father and a daughter, so lost to each other. Then I was thinking of my own father, many miles away. It had been so long since I had said, "I love you." As Janie struggled to control her tears, I breathed a prayer, "Please God, let this daughter find forgiveness." "I'm coming. Now! I'll be there in 30 minutes," she said. Click. She had hung up.

I tried to busy myself with a stack of charts on the desk. I couldn't concentrate. Room 712. I knew I had to get back to 712. I hurried down the hall nearly in a run. I opened the door. Mr. Williams lay unmoving. I reached for his pulse. There was none. "Code 99, Room 712. Code 99. Stat." The alert was shooting through the hospital within seconds after I called the switchboard through the intercom by the bed.

Mr. Williams had had a cardiac arrest. With lightning speed I leveled the bed and bent over his mouth, breathing air into his lungs. I positioned my hands over his chest and compressed. One, two, three. I tried to count. At 15 I moved back to his mouth and breathed as deeply as I could. Where was help? Again I compressed and breathed, compressed and breathed. He could not die! "O God," I prayed. "His daughter is coming. Don't let it end this way."

The door burst open. Doctors and nurses poured into the room pushing emergency equipment. A doctor took over the manual compression of the heart. A tube was inserted through his mouth as an airway. Nurses plunged syringes of medicine into the intravenous tubing. I connected the heart monitor. Nothing. Not a beat. My own heart pounded. "God, don't let it end like this. Not in bitterness and hatred. His daughter is coming. Let her find peace."

"Stand back," cried a doctor. I handed him the paddles for the electrical shock to the heart. He placed them on Mr. Williams's chest. Over and over we tried. But nothing. No response. Mr. Williams was dead. A nurse unplugged the oxygen. The gurgling stopped. One by one they left, grim and silent. How could this happen? How? I stood by his bed, stunned. A cold wind rattled the window, pelting the panes with snow. Outside, everywhere, seemed a bed of blackness, cold and dark.

How could I face his daughter? When I left the room, I saw her against a wall by a water fountain. A doctor who had been inside 712 only moments before stood at her side, talking to her, gripping her elbow. Then he moved on, leaving her slumped against the wall. Such pathetic hurt reflected from her face. Such wounded eyes. She knew. The doctor had told her that her father was gone. I took her hand and led her into the nurse's lounge. We sat on little green stools, neither saying a word. She stared straight ahead at a pharmaceutical calendar, glass-faced, almost breakable-looking.

"Janie, I'm so sorry," I said. It was pitifully inadequate. "I never hated him you know. I loved him," she said. God please help her I thought. Suddenly she whirled toward me. "I want to see him." My first thought was, "Why put yourself through more pain? Seeing him will only make it worse." But I got up and wrapped my arm around her. We walked slowly down the corridor to 712. Outside the door I squeezed her hand, wishing she would change her mind about going inside.

She pushed open the door. We moved to the bed, huddled together taking small steps in unison. Janie leaned over the bed and buried her face in the sheets. I tried not to look at her, at this sad, sad good-bye. I backed against the bedside table. My hand fell upon a scrap of yellow paper. I picked it up. It read:

My dearest Janie,
I forgive you. I pray you will also forgive me. I know that you love
me. I love you too.

Daddy

The note was shaking in my hands as I thrust it toward Janie. She read it once. Then twice. Her tormented face grew radiant. Peace began to glisten in her eyes. She hugged the scrap of paper to her breast. "Thank you, God," I whispered, looking up at the window. A few crystal stars blinked through the blackness. A snowflake hit the window and melted away, gone forever. Life seemed as fragile as a snowflake on the window. But thank you God that relationships, sometimes fragile as snowflakes, can be mended together again, but there is not a moment to spare. I crept from the room and hurried to the phone. I would call my father. I would say, "I love you."

And now a poem by an unknown author titled:

Little Things in Life

Too often we don't realize what we have until it is gone;
Too often we wait too late to say, "I'm sorry. I was wrong."
Sometimes it seems we hurt the ones we hold dearest to our hearts;
And we allow foolish things to tear our lives apart.
Far too many times we let unimportant things into our minds;

And then it's usually too late to see what made us blind.
So be sure that you let people know how much they mean to you;
Take that time to say the words before your time is through.
Be sure that you appreciate everything you've got,
And be thankful for the little things in life that mean a lot.

I will close this chapter with the Ten Commandments of Getting Ahead in Life and one of my favorite quotes.

1. Speak to people. Even if you do not know their names. Nothing is as nice as a cheerful word or greeting.
2. Smile at people. It takes 72 muscles to frown and only 14 to smile. Your smile is one of your finest assets. Use it!
3. Call people by name. The sweetest music to anyone's ears is the sound of his/her own name.
4. Be friendly and helpful. If you want to have friends, *be* one.
5. Be genuinely interested in people. If you try, you can like everybody and everybody will like you.
6. Seek out the little people. Do not limit yourself to a few friends when there are so many likable people around you.
7. Be generous with praise. And cautious with criticism. Who among us does not need the understanding and tolerance of all our friends.
8. Be considerate of the feelings of others. Usually there are three sides to a controversy—yours, the other person's and the right one.
9. Be alert to give service. What we do for others counts most in life.
10. Add to this a good sense of humor, a generous dose of patience, and a dash of humility, and you will receive many-fold blessings.

But above all else, may I suggest that:

If you could choose one characteristic that would get you through life, choose a sense of humor.

Integrity Develops Consistency

We are what we repeatedly do. Excellence then is not an act, but a habit.

This is one of my favorite chapters! It may be one of the shortest, but please don't underestimate its importance. The dictionary offers several definitions for integrity. The one I think of most often though when I hear the word is: "The quality or state of being of sound moral principle; uprightness, honesty and sincerity." I love the following quote!

Image is what people think we are.
Integrity is what we really are.

Indeed, this is so true! There are times we judge people by what we think they are rather than what they really are. The following story exemplifies this error in our ways.

A lady in a faded gingham dress and her husband, dressed in a homespun, threadbare suit, stepped off the train in Boston, and walked timidly without an appointment into the president's outer office. The secretary could tell in a moment that such backwoods, country hicks had no business at Harvard and probably didn't even deserve to be in Cambridge.

She frowned. "We want to see the president," the man said softly. "He'll be busy all day," the secretary snapped. "We'll wait," the lady replied. For hours, the secretary ignored them, hoping that the couple would finally become discouraged and go away. They didn't and the secretary grew frustrated and finally decided to disturb the president, even though it was a chore and she always regretted doing it.

"Maybe if they just see you for a few minutes, they'll leave," she told him. And he sighed in exasperation and nodded. Someone of his importance obviously didn't have the time to spend with them. He detested gingham dresses and homespun suits cluttering up his outer office. The president, stern-faced with dignity, strutted toward the couple.

The lady told him, "We had a son who attended Harvard for one year. He loved Harvard. He was happy here. But about a year ago, he was accidentally killed. And my husband and I would like to erect a memorial to him somewhere on campus."

The president wasn't touched, he was shocked. "Madam," he said gruffly, "we can't put up a statue for every person who attended Harvard and died. If we did, this place would look like a cemetery."

"Oh, no," the lady explained quickly. "We don't want to erect a statue. We thought we would like to give a building to Harvard."

The president rolled his eyes. He glanced at the gingham dress and homespun suit, then exclaimed, "A building! Do you have any earthly idea how much a building costs? We have over seven and a half million dollars in the physical plant at Harvard."

For a moment the lady was silent. The president was pleased. He could get rid of them now. And the lady turned to her husband and said quietly, "Is that all it costs to start a university? Why don't we just start our own?" Her husband nodded.

The president's face wilted in confusion and bewilderment. And Mr. and Mrs. Leland Stanford walked away, traveling to Palo Alto, California, where they established the university that bears their name, a memorial to a son that Harvard no longer cared about.

You can easily judge the character of others by how they treat those whom they assume can do nothing for them. The woman in the gingham dress knew who she was and where she was going and she did it.

A great motivational speaker, Cavett Roberts, made the following observation:

Character is the ability to carry out a good resolution long after the excitement of the moment has passed.

Another story that exemplifies integrity is one about a wise woman who was traveling in the mountains and found a precious stone in a stream. The next day she met another traveler who was hungry and the wise woman opened her bag to share her food. The hungry traveler saw the precious stone and asked the woman to give it to him. She did so without hesitation. The traveler left, rejoicing in his good fortune. He knew the stone was worth enough to give him security for a lifetime. But a few days later, he came back to return the stone to the wise woman.

"I've been thinking," he said. "I know how valuable this stone is, but I give it back in the hope that you can give me something even more precious. Give me what you have within you that enabled you to give me this stone." The hungry traveler had realized that sometimes wealth is not what you have but what's inside you that others need. Sometimes what others need is something much more substantial.

Integrity is a result of self-discipline, inner trust and a decision to be honest in all situations.

> *IT CONCERNS US TO KNOW THE PURPOSE WE SEEK IN LIFE, FOR THEN, LIKE ARCHERS AIMING AT A DEFINITE MARK, WE SHALL BE MORE LIKELY TO ATTAIN WHAT WE WANT.*
>
> *—ARISTOTLE*

What You Are

Don't determine your worth by comparing yourself with others.
It is because we are different that each of us is special.
Don't set your goals by what other people deem important.
Only you know what is best for you.
Don't take for granted the things closest to your heart;
Cling to them as you would your life, for without them life is meaningless.
Don't let your life slip through your fingers by living in the past or for the future.
By living your life one day at a time you live all the days of your life.
Don't give up when you still have something to give.
Nothing is really over until the moment you stop trying.
Don't be afraid to admit that you are less than perfect;
It is this fragile thread that binds us to each other.
Don't be afraid to encounter risks.
It is by taking chances that we learn how to be brave.
Don't shut love out of your life by saying it's impossible to find.
The quickest way to receive love is to give love.
The fastest way to lose love is to hold it too tightly.
And the best way to keep love is to give it wings.
Don't dismiss your dreams.
To be without dreams is to be without hope;
To be without hope is to be without purpose.
Don't run through life so fast that you forget not only
Where you've been but also where you're going.
Life is not a race but a journey
To be savored each step of the way.

Life is a highway. The enjoyment you get depends on the lane you choose.

John Fuhrman

Such is life but it can be so much easier if we will but learn the values in life. Included next is a list of values in life that you can easily refer back to time and time again. Highlight them so they'll be easy to find when you're scanning back through the book.

The greatest handicap—*FEAR*
The best day—*TODAY*
The hardest thing to do—*TO BEGIN*
The easiest thing to do—*FINDING FAULT*
The greatest mistake—*GIVING UP*
The greatest stumbling block—*EGOTISM*
The greatest comfort—*WORK WELL DONE*
The most disagreeable person—*THE COMPLAINER*
The worst bankruptcy—*LOSS OF ENTHUSIASM*
The greatest need—*COMMON SENSE*
The meanest feeling—*REGRET AT ANOTHER'S SUCCESS*
The best gift—*FORGIVENESS*
The hardest and most painful thing to accept—*DEFEAT*
The greatest thing—*LOVE*
The greatest success in the world—*PEACE AND SELF-FULFILLMENT*

Referring to the above list of values will help you when you are faced with what Nelson Mandela, in his 1994 Inaugural Speech, referred to as our deepest fear. This is one of my favorite quotes with a powerful message.

"Our deepest fear is not that we are inadequate. Our deepest fear is that we are powerful beyond measure. It is our light, not our darkness that most frightens us. We ask ourselves, 'Who am I to be brilliant, gorgeous, talented, fabulous?' Actually, who are you not to be? Your playing small doesn't serve the world. There's nothing enlightened about shrinking so that other people won't feel insecure around you. We are all meant to shine and we unconsciously give other people permission to do the same. As we're liberated from our own fear, our presence automatically liberates others."

Indeed, as we are liberated we will find that a lot of the things that once mattered, won't matter at all and some of the things that mattered a lot at one time, will matter less. We'll even find that some of the things that mattered before will be replaced with more meaningful concerns.

We'll realize that it doesn't matter what someone does for a living. Instead what will matter to us is whether or not they ache for, and if they dare to dream of meeting their heart's longing. How old they are won't matter to us. What will matter is whether or not they are willing to risk looking like a fool for love, for their dream, for the adventure of being alive. We won't care what planets are squaring their moon. What will matter is if they have touched the center of their own sorrow, if they have been opened by life's betrayals or if they have become shriveled and closed from fear of further pain.

We'll want to know if they can sit with pain without moving to hide it or fade it or fix it. We'll care more about whether or not they can be with joy, if they can dance with abandon and let the ecstasy fill them to the tips of their fingers and toes without cautioning them to be careful and realistic. It won't matter to us if the story they are telling is true. What will matter is whether or not they are willing to disappoint another to be true to themselves; whether or not they can bear the accusation of betrayal and yet not betray their own soul.

We'll want to know that they can see beauty even when it's not pretty everyday. We'll want to know if they can live with failure and still stand on the edge of the lake and shout to the silver of the full moon, "Yes." It won't matter to us where they live or how much money they have. What will matter is whether or not they can get up after a night of grief and despair, weary and bruised to the bone and do what needs to be done to feed the children.

It won't interest us who they know or how they came to be here. What we will want to know is whether or not they will stand beside us when times are tough and not shrink back. It won't interest us where or what or with whom they have studied. What will matter to us is what sustains them from the inside when all else falls away.

What we'll want to know is whether or not they can be alone with themselves and if they truly like the company they keep in the empty moments.

What matters most in life is that we are true to ourselves.

As the syndicated columnist Ann Landers said, "People of integrity expect to be believed. They also know time will prove them right and are willing to wait."

We can't be all things to all people. We can't do all things at once nor equally well. We can't do all things better than everyone else. We must find out who we are and be that. We have to decide what comes first and do it. We have to discover our strengths and use them. We have to learn not to compete with others because no one else is in the contest of "being you."

Certainly when we have learned these things, we will have learned to accept our own uniqueness. We will have learned to set priorities and make decisions and live with our own limitations. We will have learned to give ourselves the respect that is due and we will have become a truly vital person.

We must dare to believe that we are wonderful, unique people. That we are a once-in-history event and that it's more than a right, it's our duty to be who we are. Life is not a problem to solve but a gift to cherish. Your real riches are riches of the head and heart. True satisfaction comes from appreciating what you have, for wealth without enjoyment is of little consolation. Your real prosperity lies in being thankful. While success lies in getting what you want, true happiness lies in wanting what you get, for it is not in how much you have, but how much you enjoy.

To accomplish great things we must not only act, but also dream;
not only plan, but also believe.

The next story titled *The Lunch Bag* is a true story about Robert Fulghum and his seven-year-old daughter.

It was Molly's job to hand her father his brown paper lunch bag each morning before he headed off to work. One morning, in addition to his usual lunch bag, Molly handed him a second paper bag. This one was worn and held together with duct tape, staples and paper clips.

"Why two bags?" Fulghum asked.

"The other is something else," Molly answered.

"What's in it?"

"Just some stuff. Take it with you."

Not wanting to hold court over the matter, Fulghum stuffed both sacks into his briefcase, kissed Molly and rushed off. At midday, while hurriedly scarfing down his real lunch, he tore open Molly's bag and shook out the contents: 2 hair ribbons, 3 small stones, a plastic dinosaur, a pencil stub, a tiny seashell, 2 animal crackers, a marble, a used lipstick, a small doll, 2 chocolate kisses and 13 pennies.

Fulghum smiled, finished eating and swept the desk clean into the wastebasket—leftover lunch, Molly's junk and all.

That evening Molly ran up behind him as he read the paper. "Where's my bag?"

"What bag?"

"You know, the one I gave you this morning."

"I left it at the office. Why?"

"I forgot to put this note in it," she said. "And besides, those are my things in the sack, Daddy, the ones I really like. I thought you might like to play with them but now I want them back. You didn't lose the bag, did you Daddy?"

"Oh no," he said lying. "I just forgot to bring it home. I'll bring it tomorrow."

While Molly hugged her father's neck, he unfolded the note that had not made it into the sack: "I love you, Daddy."

Molly had given him her treasures. All that a seven-year-old held dear. Love in a paper sack and he missed it and not only had he missed it, he had thrown it away. So back to his office he went and just ahead of the night janitor, he picked up the wastebasket and poured the contents on his desk.

After washing the mustard off the dinosaurs and spraying the whole thing with breath-freshener to kill the smell of onions, he carefully smoothed out the wadded ball of brown paper, put the treasures inside and carried it home gingerly, like an injured kitten. The bag didn't look so good, but the stuff was all there and that's what counted.

After dinner he asked Molly to tell him about the stuff in the sack. It took a long time to tell. Everything had a story or a memory or was attached to dreams and imaginary friends. Fairies had brought some of the things. He had given her the chocolate kisses and she had kept them for when she needed them.

"Sometimes I think of all the times in this sweet life," Fulghum concludes the story, "when I must have missed the affection I was being given." A friend calls this "standing knee deep in a river and dying of thirst."

We should all remember that it's not the destination in life that counts, it's the journey.

The little girl smiles, the dinosaurs and chocolate kisses wrapped in old paper bags that we sometimes throw away too thoughtlessly each day, each a tiny treasure.

The journey with the people we love is all that really matters. Such a simple truth so easily forgotten. There's a beautiful poem by an unknown author titled:

Promises Kept

God never promised in whatever we do
That we'd always be happy and healthy too.
He never said that life would be free of pain,
But He said He'd be there time and again
To bolster our spirits, to lighten our way,
To give strength and courage day after day.
To make us feel worthy, to give inner peace,
And from life's tensions, a loving release.

What an incredible message! And now for one of those life's lessons that any parent can truly appreciate.

A weary mother returned from the store lugging groceries through the kitchen door. Awaiting her arrival was her eight-year-old son, anxious to relate what his younger brother had done. "While I was out playing and Dad was on a call, T.J. took his crayons and wrote on the wall! It's on the new paper you just hung in the den. I told him you'd be mad at having to do it again."

She let out a moan and furrowed her brow. "Where is your little brother right now?"

She emptied her arms with a purposeful stride. She marched to his closet where he had gone to hide. She called his full name as she entered the room. He trembled with fear; he knew that meant doom! For the next 10 minutes, she ranted and raved about the expensive wallpaper and how she had saved, lamenting on all the work it would take to repair. She condemned his actions and total lack of care. The more she scolded, the madder she got and then stomped from his room totally distraught.

She headed for the den to confirm her fears. When she saw the wall, her eyes flooded with tears for the message she read pierced her soul like a dart.

It said, "I love Mommy," surrounded by a heart.

Well the wallpaper remained, just as she found it, with an empty picture frame around it as a reminder to her and indeed to all to take time to read the handwriting on the wall.

It would do us all well to hold onto the things that really matter in life. Hold onto faith, for it is the source of believing that all things are possible—the fiber and strength of a confident soul. Hold onto hope, for it banishes doubt and enables attitudes to be positive and cheerful. Hold onto trust, for it is at the core of fruitful relationships that are secure and content. Hold onto love, for it is life's greatest gift of all for it shares, cares and gives meaning.

Hold onto family and friends, for they are the most important people in your life and they make the world a better place. They are your roots and the beginnings that you grew from; they are what has grown through time to nourish you, help you on your way and always remain close.

Hold onto all that you are and all that you have learned, for these things are what make you. Don't ignore what you feel and what you believe is right and important; your heart has a way of speaking louder than your mind.

Hold onto your dreams; achieve them honestly and diligently. Never take the easy way or submit to deceit. Remember others on your way and take time to care for their needs. Enjoy the beauty around you. Have the courage to see things differently and clearly. Make the world better one day at a time and don't let go of the important things that give meaning to your life.

There's a Chinese folk tale that illustrates the importance of persistence. In the folk tale, a holy man has a dream in which he is taken by the angels to visit heaven. As the angels escort him through the mansion they pass a room stacked full with gifts.

The holy man stops and stares at all the beautiful presents and asks, "Why are all these lovely gifts stacked up in this room?"

A beautiful angel sighs as she explains, "This is the room where we store the things people have been praying for...but sadly, they quit praying right before their presents were to be delivered."

It is sad but so true. Often the difference between success and failure is tenacity. Often we lack the tenacity to stick with it and achieve the things we dream of. To achieve the things you want in life remember the quote by the famous blues singer Janis Joplin:

Don't compromise yourself. You are all you've got.

Always listen to yourself; it is better to be wrong than simply to follow convention. If you are wrong, no matter; you have learned something and will grow stronger from it. If you are right, you have taken another step toward a fulfilling life. You can have an incredible life. It begins when you decide to take charge of your life and quit making excuses. Start by enlisting the following seven steps.

1. Be self-responsible.
2. Do what it takes to live your dreams.
3. Own your own life by having the courage to accept yourself and what you want to do.
4. Make a list of 20 or more things you'd like to accomplish.
5. Find out what motivates you deep down inside.
6. Live consistent with your own values, good morals and principles.
7. Do the things that are in your heart, not to please people but to follow your dreams.

As we come to the end of Chapter VII, recall the definition of integrity we started with: "The quality or state of being of sound moral principle; uprightness, honesty and sincerity." I would like to close with an elaboration on this definition.

As you go through life, every day you tell on yourself in a number of ways. You tell on yourself by the friends you seek, by the very manner in which you speak. You tell on yourself by the way you employ your leisure time, by the use you make of the dollar and dime. You tell on yourself by the things you wear, by the spirit in which your burdens you bear. You tell on yourself by the kind of things that make you laugh, by the records you play on your phonograph. You tell on yourself by the way you walk, by the things of which you delight to talk. You tell on yourself by the manner in which you bear defeat, by so simple a thing as how you eat. You tell on yourself by the books you choose from the well-filled shelf. In these ways and more, you tell on yourself. So remember then, there is not a particle of sense in an effort to keep up a false pretense.

Faith Builds the Vision

VIII

Cherish your visions and your dreams as they are the children of your soul; the blue print of your ultimate achievements.

Napoleon Hill

It is possible to live your dreams! Most of you reading this book bought it in the hopes that you would find somewhere in these pages the secret to an incredible life. This is a tremendous chapter and I urge you to pay particular attention to the stories, quotes and poems. Faith is one of the key steps to an incredible life. It is through faith that you will be able to build your vision of success.

How will you do that? How will you live your dreams? First you must think about, and then decide what it is you want. The beginning of any worthwhile goal or dream is always in your imagination. Then you must organize your thoughts into a definitive plan of action that you will follow to transform your dreams into reality.

Remember, your mind is your mental workshop. It is the place where you can build anything you want if you will visualize what it is; see it, feel it, taste it, believe in it. Make it something you want and truly believe in it. It is then that you will begin to develop the mental blueprint that will help you build, visualize and actualize your success. You can do it! Believe in your dream, believe in yourself and be willing to put forth the effort and an incredible life can be yours!

I Believe

I believe in miracles and dreams that will come true.
I believe in tender moments and friendship, through and through.
I believe in stardust and moonbeams all aglow.
I believe there's magic and more there than we know.
I believe in reaching out and touching from the heart.
I believe that if we touch, a gift we can impart.
I believe that if you cry, your tears are not in vain.
And when you're sad and lonely, others know your pain.
I believe that when we laugh, a sparkle starts to shine.
And I just know that spark will spread from more hearts than just mine.

I believe that hidden in the quiet of the night
There's magic, moths and gypsies.
I believe that if you dance the dances of your heart,
That greater happiness will find a brand new way to start.
I believe the gifts you have are there for you to share
And when you give them from your heart,
The whole world knows you care.

I believe that if you give even just to one,
That gift will grow in magnitude before the day is done.
I believe that comfort comes from giving part of me,
And if I share with others, there's more for all to see.

I believe that love is still the greatest gift of all
And when it's given from the heart then not one of us will fall.

There is a story about two men, both seriously ill, who occupied the same hospital room. One man was allowed to sit up in his bed for an hour each afternoon to help drain the fluid from his lungs. His bed was next to the room's only window. The other man had to spend all his time flat on his back. The men talked for hours on end. They spoke of their wives and families, their homes, their jobs, their involvement in the military service, where they had been on vacation.

And every afternoon when the man in the bed by the window could sit up, he would pass the time by describing to his roommate all the things he could see outside the window. The man in the other bed began to live for those one-hour periods where his world would be broadened and enlivened by all the activity and color of the world outside.

The window overlooked a park with a lovely lake. Ducks and swans played on the water while children sailed their model boats. Young lovers walked arm in arm amidst flowers of every color of the rainbow. Grand old trees graced the landscape and a view of the city skyline could be seen in the distance.

As the man by the window described all this in exquisite detail the man on the other side of the room would close his eyes and imagine the picturesque scene. One warm afternoon the man by the window described a parade passing by. Although the other man couldn't hear the band he could see it in his mind's eye as the gentleman by the window portrayed it with descriptive words. Days and weeks passed.

One morning, the day nurse arrived to bring water for their baths only to find the lifeless body of the man by the window who had died peacefully in his sleep. She was saddened and called the hospital attendants to take the body away. As soon as it seemed appropriate, the other man asked if he could be moved next to the window. The nurse was happy to make the switch and after making sure he was comfortable, she left him alone.

Slowly, painfully, he propped himself up on one elbow to take his first look at the world outside. Finally he would have the joy of seeing it for himself. He strained to slowly turn to look out the window beside the bed.

It faced a blank wall. The man asked the nurse what could have compelled his deceased roommate who had described such wonderful things outside this window.

The nurse responded that the man was blind and could not even see the wall. She said, "Perhaps he just wanted to encourage you." There is a tremendous happiness in making others happy despite our own situations. Shared grief is half the sorrow, but happiness when shared is doubled. Live life to its fullest. There will be challenges, there will be obstacles; they are a part of life. They are the very things that help us become who we are. There's a quote from an unknown source and a poem that both do a great job with this subject.

Take risks: If you win, you will be happy; if you lose you will be wise.

The Wind's Not Always at Our Back

The wind's not always at our back; the sky is not always blue.
Sometimes we crave the things we lack and don't know what to do.
Sometimes life's an uphill ride with mountains we must climb.
At times the river's deep and wide and crossing takes some time.

No one said that life is easy, there are no guarantees.
So trust the Lord continually on calm or stormy seas.
The challenges we face today prepare us for tomorrow.
For faith takes our fears away and peace replaces sorrow.

There will be times when you will feel your burden is more than you can bear or heavier than your neighbor's. When I was growing up, my mother was fond of saying, "God never gives you more than you can handle." Honestly, there were times I doubted her wisdom, but I usually found that she was right. Her faith and belief in times of adversity are things I have tried to remember in my adult life. The following story from an unknown author illustrates what it might be like if you could change places with your neighbor.

"Why was my burden so heavy?" I slammed the bedroom door and leaned against it. "Is there no rest from this life?" I wondered. I stumbled to my bed and dropped onto it, pressing my pillow around my ears to shut out the noise of my existence.

"Oh God," I cried, "let me sleep. Let me sleep forever and never wake up!" With a deep sob I tried to will myself into oblivion, then welcomed the blackness that came over me. Light surrounded me as I regained consciousness. I focused on its source. The figure of a man standing before a cross.

"My child," the person asked, "why did you want to come to Me before I am ready to call you?" "Lord, I'm sorry. It's just that I can't go on. You see how hard it is for me. Look at this awful burden on my back. I simply can't carry it anymore."

"But haven't I told you to cast all your burdens on Me because I care for you? My yoke is easy and My burden is light." "I knew you would say that. But why does mine have to be so heavy?"

"My child, everyone in the world has a burden. Perhaps you would like to try a different one?" "I can do that?" He pointed to several burdens lying at His feet. "You may try any of these." All of them seemed to be of equal size. But each was labeled with a name.

"There's Joan's," I said. Joan was married to a wealthy businessman. She lived in a sprawling estate and dressed her three daughters in the prettiest designer clothes. Sometimes she drove me to church in her Cadillac when my car was broken. "Let me try that one." How difficult could her burden be? I thought.

The Lord removed my burden and placed Joan's on my shoulders. I sank to my knees beneath its weight. "Take it off!" I said. "What makes it so heavy?" "Look inside." I untied the straps and opened the top. Inside was a figure of her mother-in-law and when I lifted it out, it began to speak. "Joan, you'll never be good enough for my son," it began. "He never should have married you. You're a terrible mother to my grandchildren!" I quickly placed the figure back in the pack and withdrew another. It was Donna, Joan's youngest daughter. Her head was bandaged from the surgery that had failed to resolve her epilepsy. A third figure was Joan's brother. Addicted to drugs, he had been convicted of killing a police officer. "I see why her burden is so heavy, Lord. But she's always smiling and helping others. I didn't realize!"

"Would you like to try another?" He asked quietly. I tested several. Paula's felt heavy. She was raising four small boys without a father. Debra's did too—a childhood of sexual abuse and now a marriage of emotional abuse. When I came to Ruth's burden, I didn't even try. I knew that inside I would find arthritis, old age, a demanding full-time job and a beloved husband in a nursing home. "They're all too heavy Lord," I said. "Give back my own."

As I lifted the familiar load once again, it seemed much lighter than the others. "Let's look inside." He said. I turned away, holding it close. "That's not a good idea," I said. "Why?" "There's a lot of junk in there." "Let me see." The gentle thunder of His voice compelled me.

I opened my burden. He pulled out a brick. "Tell me about this one." "Lord, You know. It's money. I know we don't suffer like people in some countries or even the homeless here in America. But we have no insurance and when the kids get sick, we can't always take them to the doctor. They've never been to a dentist. And I'm tired of dressing them in hand-me-downs." "My child, I will supply all of your needs and your children's. I've given them healthy bodies. I will teach them that expensive clothing doesn't make a person valuable in My sight."

Then He lifted out the figure of a small boy. "And this?" He asked. "Andrew." I hung my head, ashamed to call my son a burden. "But, Lord, he's hyperactive. He's not quiet like the other two. He makes me so tired. He's always getting hurt and someone is bound to think I abuse him. I yell at him all the time. Someday I may really hurt him!"

"My child," He said, "if you trust Me, I will renew your strength if you allow Me to fill you with My spirit; I will give you patience. Then He took some pebbles from my burden. "Yes, Lord," I said with a sigh. "Those are small, but they're important. I hate my hair. It's thin and I can't make it look nice. I can't afford to go to the beauty shop. I'm overweight and can't stay on a diet. I hate all my clothes. I hate the way I look."

"My child, people look at your outward appearance, but I look at your heart. By My Spirit you can gain self-control to lose weight. But your beauty should not come from outward appearance. Instead, it should come from your inner self, the unfolding beauty of a gentle and quiet spirit, which is of great worth in my sight."

My burden now seemed lighter than before. "I guess I can handle it now," I said. "There is more," He said. "Hand Me that last brick." "Oh you don't have to take that. I can handle it." "My child, give it to Me." Again His voice compelled me.

He reached out His hand and for the first time I saw the ugly wound. "But, Lord, this brick is so awful, so nasty, so...Lord! What happened to your hands? They're so scarred." No longer focused on my burden, I looked for the first time into His face. In His brow were ragged scars as though someone had pressed thorns into His flesh.

"Lord," I whispered. "What happened to you?" His loving eyes reached into my soul. "My child, you know. Hand Me the brick. It belongs to Me. I bought it." "How?" "With My blood." "But why Lord?" "Because I have loved you with an everlasting love. Give it to Me."

I placed the filthy brick into His wounded palm. It contained all the dirt and evil of my life—my pride, my selfishness, the depression that constantly tormented me. He turned to the cross and hurled my brick into the pool of blood at its base. It hardly made a ripple.

"Now My child, you need to go back. I will be with you always. When you are troubled, call to Me and I will help you and show you things you cannot imagine now." "Yes, Lord, I will call on You." I reached to pick up my burden. "You may leave that here if you wish. You see all these burdens? They are the ones that others have left at my feet. Joan's, Paula's, Debra's, Ruth's. When you leave your burdens here, I carry them with you. Remember, "My yoke is easy and My burden is light.""

As I placed my burden with Him, the light began to fade. Yet I heard Him whisper, "I will never leave you nor forsake you." A peace flooded my soul.

There will be challenges along the way and times when you feel like quitting. Success without conflict is unrealistic. Often when you do something noteworthy somebody will find fault with it so you can expect to generate a new set of tensions every time you set a new goal. Be prepared for conflict. Be a realist; be prepared for the worst.

Positive thinking is not a Pollyanna approach to life. It's an attitude that says, "I'll handle whatever comes along." If you're like me, you keep spare keys to your car and your house, just in case you misplace yours. And I for one, am certainly in favor of parachutes and escape hatches on airplanes, just in case. And I wouldn't want to be on a ship that didn't have life jackets and lifeboats. Is this negative thinking? Absolutely not! I'm making sure that if the worst were to happen, I'll survive and be able to start over again. You should do the same.

> *Before you begin a thing, remind yourself that difficulties and delays quite impossible to foresee are ahead. You can only see one thing clearly and that is your goal. Form a mental vision of that and cling to it through thick and thin.*
>
> Kathleen Norris

The more you come to understand the power of visualization, the sooner you will be on your way to success. I play golf once or twice a week with a group of friends. We are your average weekly golfers, not breaking any records but having a good time and enjoying each other's company. To shoot in the 70s is obviously not our goal but if it were, the following story demonstrates how the dream and the vision can become reality. Read the story, then decide what you want and go for it!

Major James Nesmeth had a dream of improving his golf game and he developed a unique method of achieving his goal. Until he devised this method, he was just your average weekend golfer, shooting in the mid to low 90s. Then for seven years, he quit the game completely—never touched a club, never set foot on a fairway.

Ironically, it was during this seven-year break from the game that Major Nesmeth came up with his amazingly effective technique for improving his game, a technique we can all learn from. In fact, the first time he set foot on a golf course after his hiatus from the game, he shot an astonishing 74! He had cut 20 strokes off his average without having swung a golf club in seven years! Unbelievable. Not only that, but his physical condition had actually deteriorated during those seven years.

What was Major Nesmeth's secret? Visualization. You see Major Nesmeth had spent those seven years as a prisoner of war in a cage that was approximately four and one-half feet high and five feet long.

During almost the entire time he was imprisoned, he saw no one, talked to no one, and experienced no physical activity. During the first few months he did virtually nothing but hope and pray for his release. Then he realized he had to find some way to occupy his mind or he would lose his sanity and probably his life. That's when he learned to visualize.

In his mind, he selected his favorite golf course and started playing golf. Every day, he played a full 18 holes at the imaginary country club of his dreams. He experienced everything to the last detail. He saw himself dressed in his golfing clothes. He smelled the fragrance of the trees and the freshly trimmed grass. He experienced difficult weather conditions—windy spring days, overcast winter days and sunny summer mornings. In his imagination, every detail of the tee, the individual blades of grass, the trees, the singing birds, the scampering squirrels and the lay of the course became totally real.

He felt the grip of the club in his hands. He instructed himself as he practiced smoothing out his down-swing and the follow-through on his shot. Then he watched the ball arch down the exact center of the fairway, bounce a couple of times and roll to the exact spot he had selected, all in his mind.

In the real world, he was in no hurry. He had no place to go. So in his mind he took every step on his way to the ball, just as if he were physically on the course. It took him just as long in imaginary time to play 18 holes as it would have taken in reality. Not a detail was omitted. Not once did he ever miss a shot, never a hook or slice, never a missed putt.

Seven days a week. Four hours a day. Eighteen holes. Seven years. Twenty strokes off. Shot a 74.

You say that's incredible? That's the power of vision.

Sometimes to develop a worthwhile dream, we have to break through our self-imposed limits. There's a pencil test that challenges you to connect nine dots with four lines. The dots are three rows of three dots per row. The challenge comes when you are forced to get outside the lines to connect the dots using just the four lines allowed. Try it and see how you do.

```
•   •   •
•   •   •
•   •   •
```

Before everything else, getting ready is the secret of success.

Henry Ford

You have within you the power to be all you ever dreamed of becoming. You have probably already accomplished many things in your life that you failed to recognize, deeming the accomplishment small and of little consequence. I like stories as you can tell so now I'd like to share a story with you. It's a story about three trees and their dreams.

Once upon a mountaintop, three little trees stood and dreamed of what they wanted to become when they grew up.

The first little tree looked up at the stars and said, "I want to hold treasures. I want to be covered with gold and filled with precious stones. I'll be the most beautiful treasure chest in the world!"

The second little tree looked out at the small stream trickling by on its way to the ocean. "I want to be traveling mighty waters and carrying powerful kings. I'll be the strongest ship in the world!"

The third little tree looked down into the valley below where busy men and women worked in a busy town. "I don't want to leave the mountaintop at all. I want to grow so tall that when people stop to look at me, they'll raise their eyes to heaven and think of God. I will be the tallest tree in the world."

Years passed. The rain came, the sun shone, and the little trees grew tall. One day three woodcutters climbed the mountain.

The first woodcutter looked at the first tree and said, "This tree is beautiful. It is perfect for me." With a swoop of his shining ax, the first tree fell. "Now I shall be made into a beautiful chest. I shall hold wonderful treasure!" the first tree said.

The second woodcutter looked at the second tree and said, "This tree is strong. It is perfect for me." With a swoop of his shiny ax, the second tree fell. "Now I shall sail mighty waters!" thought the second tree. "I shall be a strong ship for mighty kings."

The third tree felt her heart sink when the last woodcutter looked her way. She stood straight and tall and pointed bravely to heaven. But the woodcutter never even looked up. "Any kind of tree will do for me," he muttered. With a swoop of his ax, the third tree fell.

The first tree rejoiced when the woodcutter brought her to a carpenter's shop. But the carpenter fashioned the tree into a feedbox for animals. The once beautiful tree was not covered with gold nor with treasure. She was coated with sawdust and filled with hay for hungry farm animals.

The second tree smiled when the woodcutter took her to a shipyard, but no mighty sailing ship was made that day. Instead the once strong tree was hammered and sawed into a simple fishing boat. She was too small and too weak to sail to an ocean, or even a river; instead she was taken to a little lake.

The third tree was confused when the woodcutter cut her into strong beams and left her in a lumberyard. "What happened?" the once tall tree wondered. "All I ever wanted was to stay on the mountaintop and point to God."

Many, many days and nights passed. The three trees nearly forgot their dreams. But one night, golden starlight poured over the first tree as a young woman placed her newborn baby in the feedbox.

"I wish I could make a cradle for him," her husband whispered. The mother squeezed his hand and smiled as the starlight shone on the smooth and sturdy wood. "This manger is beautiful," she said. And suddenly the first tree knew she was holding the greatest treasure in the world.

One evening a tired traveler and his friends crowded into the old fishing boat. The traveler fell asleep as the second tree quietly sailed out into the lake. Soon a thundering and thrashing storm arose. The little tree shuddered. She knew she did not have the strength to carry so many passengers safely through with the wind and rain. The tired man awakened. He stood up, stretched out his hand and said, "Peace." The storm stopped as quickly as it had begun. And suddenly the second tree knew she was carrying the king of heaven and earth.

One Friday morning, the third tree was startled when her beam was yanked from the forgotten woodpile. She flinched as she was carried through an angry jeering crowd. She shuddered when soldiers nailed a man's hands to her. She felt ugly and harsh and cruel. But on Sunday morning, when the sun rose and the earth trembled with joy beneath her, the third tree knew God's love had changed everything. It had made the third tree strong and every time people thought of the third tree, they would think of God. That was better than being the tallest tree in the world.

So the next time you feel down because you didn't get what you wanted, just sit tight and be happy because God is thinking of something better to give you. It is not today's burdens that get to us. Rather it is the regret of yesterday and fear of tomorrow.

Regret and fear, two thieves that steal away our today. Sure, we'll make mistakes and we'll fail some too. We'll feel the strain of starting over and at times will wonder if it wasn't all in vain. I used to have such thoughts. I used to worry about the time I wasted or I thought I was wasting. Then I heard someone say that the only sure way to avoid failure was to not ever do anything. My difficult times had been my most important learning experiences. After all, it's easy to be up when everything is going your way, but it's the down times that show your true character. It's those times when it seems all is against you, that you will learn the most. When you are able to keep your hopes up in the face of adversity, you will have learned to live fully today. And today is all we really have, which brings me to the following poem by an unknown author.

Don't Look Back

As you travel through life there are always those times
when decisions just have to be made,
When the choices are hard and solutions seem scarce
and the rain seems to soak your parade!

There are some situations where all you can
do is to simply let go and move on,
Gather courage together and choose a direction
that carries you toward a new dawn.

So pack up your troubles and take a step forward
the process of change can be tough,

But think about all the excitement ahead
if you can be stalwart enough!

There could be adventures you never imagined
just waiting around the next bend,
And wishes and dreams just about to come true
in ways you can't yet comprehend!

Perhaps you'll find friendships that spring from new interests
as you challenge your status quo,
And learn there are so many options in life
and so many ways you can grow!

Perhaps you'll go places you never expected
and see things that you've never seen,
Or travel to fabulous, faraway worlds and
wonderful spots in between!

Perhaps you'll find warmth, affection and caring
a "somebody special" who's there,
To help you stay centered and listen with interest
to stories and feelings you share.

Perhaps you'll find comfort in knowing your friends
are supportive of all that you do,
And believe that whatever decisions you make
they'll be the right choices for you!

So keep putting one foot in front of the other
and taking your life day by day,
There's a brighter tomorrow that's just down the road
so don't look back, you're not going that way!

I have a friend who is such an inspiration to me. She is all the above poem describes and more! She is vibrant and alive and I relish our times together. Several years ago Madelon was diagnosed with a muscular disease that has slowed her physically, but her mind is as sharp and alert as ever. In fact, it was she who took the picture of the graduates that appears in Chapter IX as well as my picture that appears on the cover. It is to her that I dedicate the following poem.

Roses of Life

I've dreamed many dreams that never came true.
I've seen them vanish at dawn
But I've realized enough of my dreams, Thank God,
To make me want to dream on.
I've prayed many prayers when no answers came,
Though I waited patient and long.
But answers came to enough of my prayers
To make me keep praying on.
I've trusted many a friend that failed
And left me to weep alone
But I've found enough of my friends true blue
To make me keep trusting on.
I've sown many seeds that fell by the way
For the birds to feed upon
But I have held enough golden sheaves in my hands
To make me keep sowing on.
I've drained the cup of disappointment and pain
And gone many days without song
But I've sipped enough nectar from the roses of life
To make me want to live on.

And live on she does! There's a story with a moral that is told about two traveling angels. I'm not sure exactly how this story fits in here, but somehow I was compelled to include it. Maybe because there have been times in my life when I felt an angel was watching over me; maybe because of the message, for indeed, "things aren't always as they seem."

Anyway, as the story goes, the two angels stopped to spend the night in the home of a wealthy family. The family was rude and refused to let the angels stay in the mansion's guest room. Instead the angels were given a space in the cold basement. As they made their bed on the hard floor, the older angel saw a hole in the wall and repaired it. When the younger angel asked why, the older angel replied, "Things aren't always as they seem."

The next night the pair of angels came to rest at the home of a very poor, but very hospitable farmer and his wife. After sharing what little food they had, the couple let the angels sleep in their bed where they could have a good night's rest. When the sun came up the next morning, the angels found the farmer and his wife in tears. Their only cow whose milk had been their sole income, lay dead in the field.

The younger angel was infuriated and asked the older angel, "How could you have let this happen? The first man had everything, yet you helped him," she accused. "The second family had little but was willing to share everything and you let their cow die."

"Things aren't always as they seem," the older angel replied. "When we stayed in the basement of the mansion, I noticed there was gold stored in that hole in the wall. Since the owner was obsessed with greed and unwilling to share his good fortune, I sealed the wall so he wouldn't find it. Then last night as we slept in the farmer's bed, the angel of death came for his wife. I gave her the cow instead. Things aren't always as they seem."

Sometimes this is exactly what happens when things don't turn out the way they should, or the way we think they should turn out. If you have faith, you need only to trust and believe that every outcome is to your advantage. Here's a poem by an unknown author that might further help you realize this.

A Teller of Tales and a Dreamer of Dreams

A teller of tales and a dreamer of dreams,
A builder of bridges, a planner of schemes.
Could this be one person? You think it untrue?
But just look again, for that person is you!

Look back on your life and take stock of the years,
And all you accomplished through laughter and tears.
Remember the children, how they took your hand?
Remember the stories, adventures you planned?
And how you nursed someone in sickness and pain,
No thought of reward and no question of gain?

You may not feel clever, stand out in a crowd,
But count your achievements, be thankful and proud,
And look to the future, there's much to be done.
There's joy to be earned and love to be won.
Keep building your bridges and planning your schemes.
Remember that you are the weaver of dreams.

That last line makes me think of the dreamcatcher I have hanging in my bedroom window. It was a gift from my daughter for my birthday a few years back. She likes to give unique and special gifts, and as such had a friend of hers make it for me. As legend has it, the dreamcatcher keeps the bad dreams out and allows only the good ones in. I don't know, but when I dream, they're good dreams!

Decide what you want, then dream it into reality! Use these ABCs to make your dreams come true:

- Avoid negative people, places, things and habits.
- Believe in yourself.
- Consider things from every angle.
- Don't give up and don't give in.
- Enjoy life today; yesterday is gone. Tomorrow may never come!
- Family and friends are hidden treasures. Seek them and enjoy their riches.
- Give more than you planned.
- Hang on to your dreams.
- Ignore those who try to discourage you!
- Just do it!
- Keep trying no matter how hard it seems. It will get easier!
- Love yourself first and most.
- Make dreams happen.
- Never lie, cheat or steal. Always strike a fair deal.
- Open your eyes and see things as they really are.
- Practice makes perfect.
- Quitters never win and winners never quit!
- Read and learn about everything important to you.
- Stop procrastinating!
- Take control of your own destiny.
- Understand yourself in order to better understand others.
- Visualize your dreams.
- Want your dream more than anything.
- "X-ccelerate" your efforts.
- You are a unique individual. Nothing can replace *you*!
- Zero in on your goals and *go for them*!

Enthusiasm Makes the Difference

IX

One man has enthusiasm for 30 minutes, another for 30 days, but it is the man who has it for 30 years who makes a success of his life.

Edward B. Butler

As I looked through picture after picture, trying to decide on the one I felt would best depict enthusiasm, I kept coming back to the idea of a high school graduating class. The ideal picture would be one of the graduates throwing their caps in the air. This is the only picture I did not seem to have. Fortunately though, my good friend Madelon did, and she graciously consented to loan it to me. The excitement and enthusiasm is purely electric. The class has spent 18 years preparing for this day; the day they would step out of their childhood roles into the adult world that awaits them. Together they came to learn and in so doing grew together. They shared laughter, tears, hopes and dreams through the years, and developed a special bond they will share forever.

On their way to this step, they have learned a lot. They have begun to realize how everything they do affects not only their lives but others as well. They have seen how a single happy smile can readily brighten someone's day and how a little bit of thoughtfulness can show someone they care. They have learned that giving someone a helping hand or showing a friend they understand can bring happiness to them both. They have learned the power of a kind and encouraging word as they were encouraged to grow and build their dreams. Today more than ever, they understand how happiness brings happiness and loving ways bring love. They are celebrating one of life's most cherished milestones. What a wonderful exciting time!

I once told a friend of mine as we sat together at my daughter's graduation how I wished we could all have the same enthusiasm, the same excitement we had then the rest of our lives. A few years later she sent me the following award entitling me to just that!

The Bearer Is a Lifetime Member in Good Standing in the Society of Childlike Grownups and Is Hereby Entitled to:

Walk in the rain, *JUMP* in mud puddles, collect rainbows, smell flowers, blow bubbles, ooOoO, stop along the way, build sandcastles, watch the moon and stars come out.

Say *HELLO* to everyone, go barefoot, take things apart, pull the gum out of your mouth and put it back in, go on adventures, sing in the shower.

Have a merry heart, read children's books, take bubble baths, get new sneakers, hold hands and hug and kiss and dance.

Fly kites, laugh out loud, cry out loud, wander around, wonder (???) about stuff, feel happy for no reason.

Give up worry and guilt and shame, giggle and don't explain why, play tag or hide-and-seek, stay innocent, say yes and no and the magic words, ask lots of questions.

Ride bicycles, stare, take a day off but don't tell anyone, draw, paint and color, see things differently, fall down and get up again.

Talk with animals, look at the sky, kick a can around the block, sleep late, trust the universe, stay up late.

Climb trees, see wonder in a frog, take naps, do nothing, daydream.

Play with toys, play under the covers, have pillow fights, learn new stuff.

Get excited about *EVERYTHING,* be a clown, walk in puddles, play baseball, listen to music, find out how things work.

Make up rules, tell stories, believe a magician's trick, save the world, make new friends.

And do anything that brings more happiness, celebration, relaxation, communication, health, love, joy, creativity, pleasure, abundance, grace, self-esteem, courage, balance, spontaneity, passion, peace, beauty, and life energy to all human beings of this planet.

Furthermore, the above named member is officially authorized to frequent amusement parks, beaches, meadows, mountaintops, swimming pools, forests, fairs, playgrounds, picnic areas, summer camps, birthday parties, circuses, bakeries, ice cream parlors, theaters, aquariums, zoos, museums, planetariums, toy stores, festivals and other places where children of all ages gather to play and is encouraged to always remember the motto of *THE SOCIETY OF CHILDLIKE GROWNUPS:*

It's never too late to have a happy childhood and to make sure that others do too!

What exactly is enthusiasm? The dictionary defines enthusiasm as "ardent eagerness." It's the source of endless energy, the happy song in the heart. Is it any wonder then that children readily provide us the best examples of enthusiasm? They have a natural sparkle in their eyes and are unaffected by many of the things that hinder adults. They have a vibrancy, an aliveness, a natural zest for living.

The story of a little boy playing baseball is a perfect example of this type of enthusiasm. The little boy was practicing throwing the ball up and as he'd swing his bat, he'd say, "I'm going to be the best batter in the world." Time and time again, he'd throw the ball up, swing the bat and miss. But he continued saying, "I'm going to be the best batter in the world." After the third time, the young boy noticed someone watching to which he said, "Hey mister, did you see that? Three balls in the air, three strikes, no hits. I'm going to be the best pitcher in the whole wide world."

A second story demonstrates the advantages of a positive attitude and natural enthusiasm. Once there were twin brothers; one was an optimist and the other, a pessimist. On their birthday, their father decided to test their attitudes. In the pessimist room he put every new toy imaginable and in the optimist room, he put a pile of horse manure.

As soon as the pessimist saw his gifts, he began complaining. "If I ride this bike in the street I might wreck it. If I skate I might fall down and hurt myself. I know if I take this basketball outside, someone will probably steal it." He went on and on turning his birthday into doom and gloom.

When the little optimist saw the pile of horse manure with his name on it, he got excited and started running through the house looking in all the rooms, in the garage and in the backyard. Finally his dad caught him and asked him what he was looking for to which the optimist replied, "Dad, with all the horse manure you gave me, I just know there's gotta be a pony around here somewhere!"

What wonderful enthusiasm!

This final story not only demonstrates enthusiasm but determination and love as well. It particularly touches my heart since my own son is in college. It's a story about a young boy who loved football. His mother had passed away when he was very young. He was a small, thin-boned boy, but he went out for the team anyway. He made the team but never played and never missed a practice all through junior and senior high school.

His father was always there to encourage him and share in his enthusiasm for the game. Everyone on the team loved him, the coaches, his teammates. He was an inspiration to all because he never gave up even if all he accomplished was to make the team.

When he went off to college, no one thought he'd make the first string but he did. He was so excited; he called his dad and sent him season tickets to all the games. His dad never missed a game.

Then during his senior year, as he was running onto the field to practice, the coach came up to him with a telegram. It said his father had just passed away. Of course he asked the coach if he could miss the next practice. The coach said, "Sure and don't worry about the play-offs either."

The Saturday of the big play-off game came. The young man was there dressed to play. He went over to the coach telling him, "If there was ever a game I wanted to play in, this is it. Let me play coach."

Of course the coach is wondering how this young man can expect him to put in his worst player, but the young man persisted, until finally with the team behind 10 points, the coach put him in.

To everyone's amazement, the young man didn't make a single mistake. He passed, kicked, punted and caught the ball like a professional. As a matter of fact, within the last minute of the game, he caught an interception and ran it all the way back for a touchdown. The crowd went absolutely crazy.

After he went to the sidelines, the coaches and players gathered around him, saying they had never seen him play like that and the coach asked, "What happened?"

"Well coach," said the young man, "as you know my dad and I had a very special relationship. But what you didn't know coach, is that my father was also blind. This was the first time I knew he could see me play and I didn't want to let him down!" Enthusiasm had given the young man extraordinary abilities.

At times it seems children have a wisdom far beyond their years. The next story is just such an example. It was shared with me by a friend of mine.

My son Gilbert was eight years old and had been in Cub Scouts only a short time. During one of his meetings he was handed a sheet of paper, a block of wood and four tires and told to return home and give it all to "dad."

That was not an easy task for Gilbert to do. Dad was not receptive to doing things with his son. But Gilbert tried. Dad read the paper and scoffed at the idea of making a pinewood derby car with his young, eager son. The block of wood remained untouched as the weeks passed. Finally, mom stepped in to see if she could help. The project began but having no carpentry skills, I decided it would be best if I simply read the directions and let Gilbert do the work. And he did. I read aloud the measurements and the rules of what we could and couldn't do.

Within days, his block of wood was turning into a pinewood derby car. A little lopsided, but looking great (at least through the eyes of a mother). Gilbert had not seen any of the other kid's cars and was feeling pretty proud of his "Blue Lightning," the pride that comes with knowing you did something on your own.

Then the big night came. With his blue pinewood derby in his hand and pride in his heart, we headed to the big race. Once there my little one's pride turned to humility. Gilbert's car was obviously the only car made entirely on his own. All the other cars were a father-son partnership, with cool paint jobs and sleek body styles made for speed.

A few of the boys giggled as they looked at Gilbert's lopsided, wobbly, unattractive vehicle. To add to the humility, Gilbert was the only boy without a man at his side. A couple of the boys who were from single-parent homes at least had an uncle or grandfather by their side; Gilbert had "mom."

As the race began it was done in elimination fashion. You kept racing as long as you were the winner. One by one the cars raced down the finely sanded ramp. Finally it was between Gilbert and the sleekest, fastest looking car there. As the last race was about to begin, my wide-eyed, shy eight-year-old asked if they could stop the race for a minute because he wanted to pray. The race stopped.

Gilbert hit his knees clutching his funny looking block of wood between his hands. With a wrinkled brow he set to converse with his Father. He prayed in earnest for a very long minute and a half. Then he stood and with a smile on his face announced, "Okay, I am ready."

As the crowd cheered, a boy named Tommy stood with his father as their car sped down the ramp. Gilbert stood with his Father within his heart and watched his block of wood wobble down the ramp with surprisingly great speed and rushed over the finish line a fraction of a second before Tommy's car.

Gilbert leaped into the air with a loud "thank you" as the crowd roared in approval. The scout master came up to Gilbert with the microphone in his hand and asked the obvious question, "So you prayed to win, huh Gilbert?"

To which my young son answered, "Oh, no sir. That wouldn't be fair to ask God to help you beat someone else. I just asked Him to make it so I didn't cry when I lost."

Gilbert didn't ask God to win the race. He didn't ask God to fix the outcome. Gilbert asked God to give him strength in the outcome. Gilbert's simple prayer spoke volumes to those present that night. He never doubted that God would indeed answer his request. Gilbert walked away a winner that night, with his Father at his side.

Life is a series of experiences, each one of which makes us bigger, even though sometimes it is hard to realize this.

Henry Ford

As you read the next story you may initially wonder how it fits into a chapter on enthusiasm. Let me remind you, enthusiasm gives us extraordinary abilities and this story is an incredible demonstration of that.

Lisa sat on the floor of her old room, staring at the box that lay in front of her. It was an old shoe box that she had decorated to become a memory box many years before. Stickers and penciled flowers covered the top and sides. Its edges were worn, the corners of the lid taped so as to keep their shape.

It had been three years since Lisa last opened the box. A sudden move to Boston had kept her from packing it. But now that she was back home, she took the time to look again at the memories. Fingering the corners of the box and stroking its cover, Lisa pictured in her mind what was inside.

There was a photo of the family trip to the Grand Canyon, a note from her friend telling her that Nick Bicotti liked her, and the Indian arrowhead she had found while on her senior class trip. One by one she remembered the items in the box, lingering over the sweetest, until she came to the last and only painful memory. She knew what it looked like: a single sheet of paper upon which lines had been drawn to form boxes, 490 of them to be exact. And each box contained a check mark, one for each time. And now for the story behind it.

"How many times must I forgive my brother?" the disciple Peter had asked Jesus. "Seven times?" Lisa's Sunday school teacher had read Jesus' surprise answer to the class. "Seventy times seven."

Lisa had leaned over to her brother Brent as the teacher continued reading. "How many times is that?" she whispered. Brent though two years younger was smarter than she was. "Four hundred and ninety," Brent wrote on the corner of his Sunday school paper. Lisa saw the message, nodded and sat back in her chair. She watched her brother as the lesson continued. He was small for his age, with narrow shoulders and short arms. His glasses were too large for his face and his hair always matted in swirls. He bordered on being a nerd, but his incredible skills at everything, especially music, made him popular with his classmates.

Brent had learned to play the piano at age four, the clarinet at age seven and had just begun to play oboe. His music teachers said he'd be a famous musician someday. There was only one thing at which Lisa was better than Brent and that was basketball. They played it almost every afternoon after school. Brent could have refused to play but he knew it was Lisa's only joy in the midst of her struggles to get Cs and Ds at school.

Lisa's attention came back to her Sunday school teacher as the woman finished the lesson and closed with a prayer. That same Sunday afternoon found brother and sister playing basketball in the driveway. It was then that the counting had begun. Brent was guarding Lisa as she dribbled toward the basket. He had tried to bat the ball away, got his face near her elbow and took a shot on the chin. "Ow!" he cried out and turned away.

Lisa saw her opening and drove to the basket, making an easy layup. She gloated over her success but stopped when she saw Brent. "You okay?" she asked. Brent shrugged his shoulders. "Sorry," Lisa said. "Really it was a cheap shot." "It's all right. I forgive you," he said. A thin smile then formed on his face. "Just 489 more times though."

"Whaddaya mean?" Lisa asked. "You know what we learned in Sunday school today. You're supposed to forgive someone 490 times. I just forgave you, so now you have 489 left," he kidded. The two of them laughed at the thought of keeping track of every time Lisa had done something to Brent. They were sure she had gone past 490 long ago. The rain interrupted their game and the two moved indoors.

"Wanna play battleship?" Lisa asked. Brent agreed and they were soon on the floor of the living room with their game boards in front of them. Each took turns calling out a letter and number combination hoping to hit each other's ships. Lisa knew she was in trouble as the game went on. Brent had only lost one ship out of five. Lisa had lost three. Desperate to win, she found herself leaning over the edge of Brent's barrier ever so slightly. She was thus able to see where Brent had placed two of his ships. She quickly evened the score.

Pleased, Lisa searched once more for the location of the last two ships. She peered over the barrier again, but this time Brent caught her in the act. "Hey, you're cheating!" He stared at her in disbelief. Lisa's face turned red, her lips quivered. "I'm sorry," she said staring at the carpet. There was not much Brent could say. He knew Lisa sometimes did things like this. He felt sorry that Lisa found so few things she could do well. It was wrong for her to cheat but he knew the temptation was hard for her. "Okay, I forgive you," Brent said. Then he added with a small laugh, "I guess it's down to 488 now, huh?" "Yeah, I guess so." She returned his kindness with a weak smile and added, "Thanks for being my brother, Brent."

Brent's forgiving spirit gripped Lisa and she wanted him to know how sorry she was. It was that evening that she had made the chart with the 490 boxes. She showed it to him before he went to bed. "We can keep track of every time I mess up and you forgive me," she said. "See, I'll put a check in each box like this." She placed two marks in the upper left-hand boxes. "These are for today." Brent raised his hands to protest. "You don't need to keep..." "Yes I do!" Lisa interrupted. "You're always forgiving me and I want to keep track. Just let me do this!" She went back to her room and tacked the chart to her bulletin board.

There were many opportunities to fill in the chart in the years that followed. She once told the kids at school that Brent talked in his sleep and called out Rhonda Hill's name, even though it wasn't true. The teasing caused Brent days and days of misery. When she realized how cruel she had been, Lisa apologized sincerely. That night she marked box number 96.

Forgiveness 211 came in the tenth grade when Lisa failed to bring home his English book. Brent had stayed home sick that day and had asked her to bring it so he could study for a quiz. She forgot and he got a C. Number 393 was for lost keys, 418 for the extra bleach she put in the washer, which ruined his favorite polo shirt and 449 for the dent she put in his car when she borrowed it.

There was a small ceremony when Lisa checked number 490. She used a gold pen for the check mark, had Brent sign the chart and then placed it in her memory box. "I guess that's the end," Lisa said. "No more screwups from me anymore!" Brent just laughed. "Yeah right!" Number 491 was just another one of Lisa's careless mistakes but its hurt lasted a lifetime.

Brent had become all that his music teachers said he would. Few could play the oboe better than he. In his fourth year at the best music school in the United States, he received the opportunity of a lifetime, a chance to try out for the New York City's great orchestra. The tryout would be held sometime during the following two weeks. It would be the fulfillment of his young dreams. But he never got the chance.

Brent had been out when the call about the tryout came to the house. Lisa was the only one home and on her way out the door, eager to get to work on time. "Two-thirty on the tenth," the secretary said on the phone. Lisa did not have a pen but she told herself she could remember it. "Got it. Thanks." I can remember that, she thought. But she did not.

It was a week later around the dinner table that Lisa realized her mistake. "So, Brent," his mom asked him, "when do you try out?" "Don't know yet. They're supposed to call." Lisa froze in her seat. "Oh no!" she blurted out loud. "What's today's date? Quick!" "It's the twelfth," her dad answered. "Why?"

A terrible pain ripped through Lisa's heart. She buried her face in her hands, crying. "Lisa, what's the matter," her mother asked. Through sobs Lisa explained what had happened. "It was two days ago. The tryout. Two-thirty. The call came last week." Brent sat back in his chair not believing Lisa. "Is this one of your jokes, sis?" he asked though he could tell her misery was real. She shook her head, still unable to look at him. "Then I really missed it?" She nodded.

Brent ran out of the kitchen without a word. He did not come out of his room the rest of the evening. Lisa tried once to knock on the door but she could not face him. She went to her room where she cried bitterly. Suddenly she knew what she needed to do. She had ruined Brent's life. He could never forgive her for that. She had failed her family and there was nothing to do but leave home. Lisa packed her pickup truck in the middle of the night and left a note behind, telling her folks she'd be all right. She began writing a note to Brent but her words sounded empty to her. Nothing I say could make a difference anyway, she thought.

Two days later she got a job as a waitress in Boston. She found an apartment not too far from the restaurant. Her parents tried many times to reach her but Lisa ignored their letters. "It's too late," she wrote them once. "I've ruined Brent's life and I'm not coming back."

Lisa did not think she would ever see home again. But one day in the restaurant where she worked she saw a face she knew. "Lisa!" said Mrs. Nelson, looking up from her plate. "What a surprise." The woman was a friend of Lisa's family from back home. "I was so sorry to hear about your brother," Mrs. Nelson said softly. "Such a terrible accident but we can all be thankful that he died quickly. He didn't suffer." Lisa stared at the woman in shock.

"Wh-hat?" she finally stammered. It couldn't be! Her brother? Dead? The woman quickly saw that Lisa did not know about the accident. She told the girl the sad story of the speeding car, the rush to the hospital, the doctors working over Brent. But all they could do was not enough to save him. Lisa returned home that afternoon.

Now she found herself in her room thinking about her brother as she held the small box that held some of her memories of him. Sadly, she opened the box and peered inside. It was as she remembered, except for one item, Brent's chart. It was not there. In its place, at the bottom of the box, was an envelope. Her hand shook as she tore it open and removed a letter. The first page read:

Dear Lisa,
 It was you who kept count, not me. But if you're stubborn enough to keep count, use the new chart I've made for you.
             Love,
             Brent

Lisa turned to the second page where she found a chart just like the one she had made as a child, but on this one the lines were drawn in perfect precision. And unlike the chart she had kept, there was but one check mark in the upper left-hand corner. Written in red felt-tip pen over the entire page were the words: "Number 491. Forgiven forever."

What an extraordinary person that young man was. I have a mug from my son that says *#1 MOM* that he gave me when he was in high school. It means the world to me, in fact the writing is barely legible with the years. I also have a mug from my daughter that has a picture of a mama bear holding a baby bear's hand with the caption that reads, "A mother holds her children's hands for awhile; their hearts forever." She knows. She is a mother herself now. Most likely the mother of the young man in the above story felt exactly as the following poem describes and the day will come when my daughter will too. I know. I've been there!

A Touch of Love

You were six months old and full of fun,
With a blink of my eye you were suddenly one.
There were so many things we were going to do,
But I turned my head and you turned two.
At two, you were very dependent on me,
But independence took over when you turned three.
Your third birthday, another year I tried to ignore,
But when I lit the candles, there weren't three but four.
Four was the year that you really strived.
Why look at you now, you're already five.
Now you are ready for books and for rules,
This is the year you go to school.

> The big day came, you were anxious to go,
> We walked to the bus going oh so slow.
> As you climbed aboard and waved good-bye,
> I felt a lump in my throat and tears stung my eyes.
> Time goes so fast, it's hard to believe
> That just yesterday you were home here with me.
> And tomorrow when you come home and I see you jump to the ground
> You'll be wearing your cap and graduation gown.
> So I'm holding to these moments as hard as I can,
> Because the next time I look, I'll be seeing a man.

As the seasons pass and our lives change, we grow in age and wisdom and like the graduates at the beginning of this chapter we continue learning. We learn courage as we stand up for what we believe in and determination when we do what's in our hearts. We learn to smile on the outside when inside we may feel like crying for the sake of supporting a friend or loved one. We learn compassion for others and empathy for their needs. We learn to do more than is expected at times without complaining and willingly stand by our friends in their times of need, selflessly expecting nothing in return. We understand the meaning of loyalty. We develop confidence on our walk through life and when life seems to be falling apart at our feet, we learn to look forward to a brighter tomorrow. We never give up learning and growing and reaching. And if we're fortunate, we never lose our youthful enthusiasm.

Life's Seasons

> There's a season for beginnings when the world is fresh and new,
> When we shape our dreams of all the things we plan and hope to do.
>
> A season for maturing when we think and work and grow,
> And a season for the harvesting of all we've come to know.
>
> And each successive season grows richer than the last,
> As treasures of the present add to memories of the past.
>
>   Author unknown

Today is the day to decide to be happy, to have the incredible life you want. I will therefore conclude this chapter with a list of reminders because right now...

- Somebody is thinking of you.
- Somebody is caring about you.
- Somebody misses you.
- Somebody wants to talk to you.
- Somebody wants to be with you.
- Somebody hopes you aren't in trouble.
- Somebody is thankful for the support you have provided.
- Somebody wants to hold your hand.
- Somebody hopes everything turns out all right.
- Somebody wants you to be happy.
- Somebody wants you to find him/her.
- Somebody is celebrating your successes.
- Somebody wants to give you a gift.
- Somebody thinks that you *are* a gift.
- Somebody hopes you're not too cold or too hot.
- Somebody wants to hug you.
- Somebody loves you.
- Somebody wishes you would lavish them with small things.
- Somebody admires your strength.
- Somebody is thinking of you and smiling.
- Somebody wants to be your shoulder to cry on.
- Somebody wants to go out with you and have a lot of fun.
- Somebody thinks the world of you.
- Somebody wants to protect you.
- Somebody would do anything for you.
- Somebody wants to be forgiven.
- Somebody is grateful for your forgiveness.
- Somebody wants to laugh with you about old times.
- Somebody remembers you and wishes that you were there.
- Somebody is praising God for you.
- Somebody needs to know that your love is unconditional.
- Somebody values your advice.
- Somebody wants to tell you how much he/she cares.
- Somebody wants to stay up watching old movies with you.
- Somebody wants to share his/her dreams with you.
- Somebody wants to hold you in his/her arms.
- Somebody wants *you* to hold him/her in your arms.
- Somebody treasures your spirit.
- Somebody wishes he/she could *stop* time because of you.
- Somebody praises God for your friendship and love.

- Somebody can't wait to see you.
- Somebody wishes that things didn't have to change.
- Somebody loves you for who you are.
- Somebody loves the way you make him/her feel.
- Somebody is hoping he/she can grow old with you.
- Somebody hears a song that reminds him/her of you.
- Somebody wants you to know he/she is there for you.
- Somebody's glad that you're his/her friend.
- Somebody wants to be your friend.
- Somebody stayed up all night thinking about you.
- Somebody is alive because of you.
- Somebody is very remorseful after losing your friendship.
- Somebody is wishing that you noticed him/her.
- Somebody wants to get to know you better.
- Somebody believes that you are his/her soul mate.
- Somebody wants to be near you.
- Somebody misses your advice/guidance.
- Somebody has faith in you.
- Somebody trusts you.
- Somebody needs you to send him/her a letter or postcard.
- Somebody needs your support.
- Somebody needs you to have faith in him/her.
- Somebody will cry when he/she reads this.
- Somebody needs you to let him/her be your friend.

Yes, somebody needs you to let him/her be your friend...read on.

One day, when I was a freshman in high school, I saw a kid from my class walking home from school. His name was Kyle. It looked like he was carrying all of his books. I thought to myself, "Why would anyone bring home all his books on a Friday? He must really be a nerd." I had quite a weekend planned (parties and a football game with my friends tomorrow afternoon), so I shrugged my shoulders and went on. As I was walking, I saw a bunch of kids running toward him.

They ran at him, knocking all his books out of his arms and tripping him so he landed in the dirt. His glasses went flying, and I saw them land in the grass about 10 feet from him. He looked up and I saw this terrible sadness in his eyes. My heart went out to him. So, I jogged over to him and as he crawled around looking for his glasses, I saw a tear in his eye. As I handed him his glasses, I said, "Those guys are jerks. They really should get lives." He looked at me and said, "Hey, thanks!" There was a big smile on his face. It was one of those smiles that showed real gratitude.

I helped him pick up his books, and asked him where he lived. As it turned out, he lived near me, so I asked him why I had never seen him before. He said he had gone to private school before now.

I asked him if he wanted to play football on Saturday with me and my friends. He said yes. We hung out all weekend and the more I got to know Kyle, the more I liked him. And my friends thought the same of him. Monday morning came, and there was Kyle with the huge stack of books again. I stopped him and said, "Boy, you are gonna build some serious muscles with this pile of books everyday!" He just laughed and handed me half the books.

Over the next four years, Kyle and I became best friends. When we were seniors, we began to think about college. Kyle decided on Georgetown, and I was going to Duke. I knew that we would always be friends, that the miles would never be a problem. He was going to be a doctor, and I was going for business on a football scholarship. Kyle was valedictorian of our class. I teased him all the time about being a nerd.

On graduation day, I saw Kyle. He looked great. He was one of those guys that really found himself during high school. He filled out and actually looked good in glasses. He had more dates than I and all the girls loved him! Boy, sometimes I was jealous. Today was one of those days. I could see that he was nervous about his speech. So, I smacked him on the back and said, "Hey, big guy, you'll be great!" He looked at me with one of those looks (the really grateful one) and smiled. "Thanks," he said.

As he started his speech, he cleared his throat, and began. "Graduation is a time to thank those who helped you make it through those tough years, your parents, your teachers, your siblings, maybe a coach... but mostly your friends. I am here to tell all of you that being a friend to someone is the best gift you can give. I am going to tell you a story." I just looked at my friend with disbelief as he told the story of the first day we met. He had planned to kill himself over the weekend. He talked of how he had cleaned out his locker so his mom wouldn't have to do it later and was carrying his stuff home. He looked hard at me and gave me a little smile. "Thankfully, I was saved. My friend saved me from doing the unspeakable." I heard the gasp go through the crowd as this handsome, popular boy told us all about his weakest moment. I saw his mom and dad looking at me and smiling that same grateful smile. Not until that moment did I realize its depth. Never underestimate the power of your actions. With one small gesture you can change a person's life.

It's Your Life... You Decide! X

The key to happiness is having dreams.
The key to success is making them come true.

One of my favorite poems is *Footprints*. I have it hanging in my upstairs bath, on a shelf in my family room and it even embellishes a throw I cover with when watching TV in the evenings. Often when I walk along the beach, I look back at my own footprints and the poem crosses my mind. This is the last chapter of *Life's Incredible* and the last of the 10 Key Steps. I can't think of a better way to begin this last chapter than with the poem.

Footprints

One night a man had a dream.
He dreamed he was walking along the beach with the Lord.
Across the sky flashed scenes from his life.
On each scene, he noticed two sets of footprints in the sand;
One belonging to him and the other to the Lord.
When the last scene of his life flashed before him,
He looked back at the footprints in the sand.
He noticed that many times along the path of his life there was only one set of footprints.
He also noticed that it happened at the very lowest and saddest times of his life.
This really bothered him and he questioned the Lord about it.
"Lord you said that once I decided to follow you, you'd walk with me all the way.
But I have noticed that during the most troublesome times in my life, there is only one set of footprints.
I don't understand why when I need you most you would leave me.
The Lord replied, "My precious, precious child, I love you and I would never leave you.
During the times of trial and suffering when you see only one set of footprints, it was then that I carried you.

What a wonderful sentiment to know that you are not alone. There is always someone there to love, encourage, and support you. And who you are does make a difference.

A teacher in New York decided to honor each of her seniors in high school by telling them the difference they each made. Using a process developed by Helice Bridges of Del Mar, California, she called each student to the front of the class, one at a time. First, she told them how the student made a difference to her and the class. Then she presented each of them with a blue ribbon imprinted with white letters that read, "Who I Am Makes a Difference."

Afterwards the teacher decided to do a class project to see what kind of impact recognition would have on a community. She gave each of the students three more ribbons and instructed them to go out and spread this acknowledgment ceremony. Then they were to follow up on the results, see who honored whom and report back to the class in about a week.

One of the boys in the class went to a junior executive in a nearby company and honored him for helping him with his career planning. He gave him a blue ribbon and put it on his shirt. Then he gave him two extra ribbons and said, "We're doing a class project on recognition and we'd like you to go out and find somebody to honor, give them a blue ribbon, then give them the extra blue ribbon so they can acknowledge a third person to keep this acknowledgment ceremony going. Then please report back to me and tell me what happened."

Later that day, the junior executive went in to see his boss, who had been noted, by the way, to be a kind of grouchy fellow. He sat his boss down and he told him that he deeply admired him for being a creative genius. The boss seemed very surprised. The junior executive asked him if he would accept the gift of the blue ribbon and would he give him permission to put it on him. His surprised boss said, "Well, sure."

The junior executive took the blue ribbon and placed it right on his boss's jacket above his heart. As he gave him the last extra ribbon, he said, "Would you do me a favor? Would you take this extra ribbon and pass it on by honoring somebody else? The young boy who first gave me the ribbons is doing a project in school and we want to keep this recognition ceremony going and find out how it affects people."

That night the boss came home to his 14-year-old son and sat him down. He said, "The most incredible thing happened to me today. I was in my office and one of the junior executives came in and told me he admired me and gave me a blue ribbon for being a creative genius. Imagine. He thinks I'm a creative genius. Then he put this blue ribbon that says, 'Who I Am Makes a Difference' on my jacket above my heart. He gave me an extra ribbon and asked me to find somebody else to honor. As I was driving home tonight, I started thinking about whom I would honor with this ribbon and I thought about you. I want to honor you."

"My days are really hectic and when I come home I don't pay a lot of attention to you. Sometimes I scream at you for not getting good enough grades in school and for your bedroom being a mess, but somehow tonight, I just wanted to sit here and well, just let you know that you do make a difference to me. Besides your mother, you are the most important person in my life. You're a great kid and I love you!"

The startled boy started to sob and sob and he couldn't stop crying. His whole body shook. He looked up at his father and said through his tears, "I was planning on committing suicide, Dad, because I didn't think you loved me. Now I don't need to."

What an incredible message.

> ### WHO I AM MAKES A DIFFERENCE BECAUSE I AM A PERSON WITH A HEART, AND FEELINGS AND WITH A NEED TO BE ACCEPTED.

What a difference a little encouragement can make to a person. Have you ever noticed what negative peer pressure can do? Go down to the fish market some day and look into the crab barrel. They never have to put a lid on it because if one crab starts to crawl out, the others will grab on to him and pull him back down. That's what negative peer pressure does.

There's a story about a group of frogs who were traveling through the woods when two of them fell into a deep pit. The other frogs gathered around and saw how deep the pit was. They told the two frogs they were as good as dead but the two frogs ignored the comments and tried to jump out of the pit with all of their might. The other frogs kept telling them to stop, saying they were as good as dead.

Finally, one of the frogs took heed to what the other frogs were saying and gave up. He fell down and died. The other frog continued to jump as hard as he could. Once again, the crowd of frogs yelled at him to stop the pain and just die. He jumped even harder and finally made it out.

When he got out, the other frogs said, "Didn't you hear us?" The frog explained to them that he was deaf. He thought they were encouraging him the entire time.

This story teaches two lessons. There is power of life and death in the tongue. An encouraging word to someone who is down can lift them up and help them make it through the day. So be careful what you say. Speak well of those who cross your path. An encouraging word can go such a long way.

Sometimes we don't realize our own potential until someone points it out to us. Perhaps up to this point you haven't realized yours. It's possible you've been like the young lion cub in my grandson's favorite movie, "The Lion King." In the movie, there's a scene where the young lion king, Simba, is living in exile, trying to avoid adult responsibilities by escaping into a life of meaningless leisure with Timon, the meekrat and Pumba, the warthog.

One day Simba is drinking from the stream and he is confronted with a vision of his late father, King Mufasa who challenges him by saying, "Simba, you have forgotten who you are. Look inside yourself. You are more than what you have become."

Are you more than what you have become? The best day of your life will be the one on which you decide your life is your own. No apologies, no excuses. No one to lean on, rely on, or blame. I urge you; decide today to take responsibility for the quality of your life. You'll be glad you did!

There will be times when a simple action or something that you think is unimportant can change another person's life or thinking. A friend shared the following thoughts with me.

Life isn't about keeping score.
It's not about how many friends you have or how accepted you are.
About whether you have plans this weekend or if you're alone.
It isn't about who you're dating, who you used to date, how many people
    you've dated or if you haven't dated anyone at all.
It isn't about who you've kissed; it isn't about sex.
It isn't about who your family is or how much money they have or what
    kind of car you drive or where you are sent to school.
It's not about how beautiful or ugly you think you are.
Or what clothes you wear, what shoes you have on, or what kind of music
    you like.
It's not about if your hair is blonde, red, black or brown; or if your skin is
    too light or too dark.
Not about what grades you get, how smart you are, how smart everybody
    else thinks you are, or how smart standardized tests say you are.

It's not about what clubs you're in or how good you are at your sport.
It's not about representing your whole being on a piece of paper and see-
ing who will "accept the written you." Life is so much more.
To truly live you must:
Be understanding to your enemies, be loyal to your friends.
Be strong enough to face the world each day but weak enough to know you
can't do everything alone.
Be generous to those who need your help, be frugal with what you need
yourself.
Be wise enough to know that you do not know everything.
Be foolish enough to believe in miracles.
Be willing to share your joys with others, be willing to share your sorrows
with others.
Be a leader when you see a path others have missed, be a follower when
you are shrouded by the mists of uncertainty.
Be the first to congratulate an opponent who succeeds, be the last to criti-
cize a colleague who fails.
Be sure where your next step will fall so that you will not tumble.
Be sure of your final destination in case you are going the wrong way.
Be loving to those who love you.
Be loving to those who do not love you and they may change.
Above all, be yourself.

*Your chances of success in any undertaking can always be mea-
sured by your belief in yourself.*

Robert Collier

There will be challenges and obstacles for you to overcome. They are
a part of life. To evade them is to do nothing. Each time we meet a challenge and overcome it, we experience personal satisfaction and enhanced
self-esteem. In fact, often our most incredible victories are accompanied
by intense pain.

My son's tennis match mentioned in a previous chapter is just such an
example. In spite of the incredible pain of not only leg cramps but stomach cramps as well, and bordering on dehydration, he didn't quit. It's true
the final score didn't show him as the winner but he had won. He had won
a personal victory. The endurance to continue the match in spite of the
intense pain made him a winner that day.

My 16-year-old son had proven to himself more than anyone else that
he was capable of going beyond what he may have previously considered
his limits of endurance to achieve a higher purpose. As I watched my son

that day and in many matches that followed, the words of Theodore Roosevelt came to mind when he said, "It is not the critic who counts; nor the man who points out how the strong man stumbled, or where the doer of deed could have done better."

"The credit belongs to the man who is actually in the arena; whose face is marred by dust and sweat and blood; who strives valiantly; who errs and comes up short again and again; who knows the great enthusiasms, great devotions, and spends himself in a worthy cause."

"Who at the best knows in the end the triumph of high achievement; and who at the worst, if he fails, at least fails while daring greatly; so that his place shall never be with those cold and timid souls who know neither victory nor defeat."

What an incredible message from one of the great leaders of our country. And now for a poem by an unknown author.

When Things Go Wrong

When things go wrong as they sometimes will,
When the road you're trudging seems all uphill,
When the funds are low and the debts are high,
And you want to smile but you have to sigh,
When care is pressing you down a bit,
Rest if you must, but don't you quit.

Life is strange with its twists and turns,
As everyone of us sometimes learns,
And many a failure turns about,
When he might have won had he stuck it out;
Don't give up though the pace seems slow,
You may succeed with another blow.

Success is failure turned inside out,
The silver tint of the clouds of doubt,
And you can never tell how close you are,
It may be near when it seems so far;
So stick to the fight when you're hardest hit,
It's when things seem worst that you must not quit.

> ### MEN DO NOT DECIDE THEIR FUTURE.
> ### THEY DECIDE THEIR HABITS AND THEIR HABITS
> ### DECIDE THEIR FUTURE.

In a university commencement address several years ago, Brian Dyson, CEO of Coca Cola Enterprises, spoke of the relation of work to one's other commitments. "Imagine life as a game in which you are juggling some five balls in the air. You name them—work, family, health, friends and spirit—and you're keeping all these balls in the air. You will soon understand that work is a rubber ball. If you drop it, it will bounce back. But the other four balls, family, health, friends and spirit are made of glass. If you drop one of these, they will be irrevocably scuffed, marked, nicked, damaged or even shattered. They will never be the same. You must understand that and strive for balance in your life." How?

Don't undermine your worth by comparing yourself with others. It is because we are different that each of us is special.

Don't set your goals by what other people deem important. Only you know what is best for you.

Don't take for granted the things closest to your heart. Cling to them as you would your life, for without them, life is meaningless.

Don't let your life slip through your fingers by living in the past or in the future. By living your life one day at a time, you live *all* the days of your life.

Don't give up when you still have something to give. Nothing is really over until the moment you stop trying.

Don't be afraid to admit that you are less than perfect. It is this fragile thread that binds us to each other.

Don't be afraid to encounter risks. It is by taking chances that we learn how to be brave.

Don't shut love out of your life by saying it is impossible to find. The quickest way to receive love is to give love; the fastest way to lose love is to hold it too tightly; and the best way to keep love is to give it wings.

Don't dismiss your dreams. To be without dreams is to be without hope. To be without hope is to be without purpose.

Don't run through life so fast that you forget not only where you have been, but also where you are going. Life is not a race, but a journey to be savored each step of the way.

Don't forget, a person's greatest emotional need is to feel appreciated.

Don't be afraid to learn. Knowledge is weightless, a treasure you can always carry easily.

Don't use time or words carelessly. Neither can be retrieved.

Yesterday is history, tomorrow is a mystery but today is a gift; that's why we call it the present.

Great, great words of wisdom. And now for a speech that was never actually given but received a lot of attention when it was first introduced and recently has even been put to music and read over the radio. The author is unknown.

Ladies and gentlemen of the class of '97:

Wear sunscreen.

If I could offer you only one tip for the future, sunscreen would be it. The long-term benefits of sunscreen have been proven by scientists, whereas the rest of my advice has no basis more reliable than my own meandering experience. I will dispense this advice now.

Enjoy the power and beauty of your youth. Oh, never mind. You will not understand the power and beauty of your youth until they've faded. But trust me, in 20 years, you'll look back at photos of yourself and recall in a way you can't grasp now how much possibility lay before you and how fabulous you really looked. You are not as fat as you imagine.

Don't worry about the future, but know that worrying is as effective as trying to solve an algebra equation by chewing bubble gum. The real troubles in your life are apt to be things that never crossed your worried mind, the kind that blindside you at four o'clock on some idle Tuesday.

Do one thing everyday that scares you.

Sing.

Don't be reckless with other people's hearts. Don't put up with people who are reckless with yours.

Floss.

Don't waste time on jealousy. Sometimes you're ahead, sometimes you're behind. The race is long and in the end, it's only with yourself.

Remember compliments you receive. Forget the insults. If you succeed in doing this, tell me how.

Keep your old love letters. Throw away your old bank statements.

Stretch.

Don't feel guilty if you don't know what you want to do with your life. The most interesting people I know didn't know at 22 what they wanted to do with their lives. Some of the most interesting 40-year-olds I know still don't.

Get plenty of calcium. Be kind to your knees. You'll miss them when they're gone.

Maybe you'll marry, maybe you won't. Maybe you'll have children, maybe you won't. Maybe you'll divorce at 40, maybe you'll dance the funky chicken on your 75th wedding anniversary. Whatever you do, don't congratulate yourself too much, or berate yourself either. Your choices are half chance. So are everybody else's.

Enjoy your body. Use it every way you can. Don't be afraid of it or of what other people think of it. It's the greatest instrument you'll ever own.

Dance, even if you have nowhere to do it but your living room.

Read the directions, even if you don't follow them.

Do not read beauty magazines. They will only make you feel ugly.

Get to know your parents. You never know when they'll be gone for good.

Be nice to your other siblings. They're your best link to your past and the people most likely to stick with you in the future.

Understand that friends come and go, but with a precious few you should hold on. Work hard to bridge the gaps in geography and lifestyle, because the older you get, the more you need the people who knew you when you were young.

Live in New York once, but leave before it makes you hard. Live in Northern California once, but leave before it makes you soft. Travel.

Accept certain inalienable truths. Prices will rise. Politicians will philander. You, too, will get old. And when you do, you'll fantasize that when you were young, prices were reasonable, politicians were noble and children respected their elders.

Respect your elders.

Don't expect anyone else to support you. Maybe you have a trust fund. Maybe you'll have a wealthy spouse. But you never know when either one might run out.

Don't mess too much with your hair or by the time you're 40 it will look 85.

Be careful whose advice you buy, but be patient with those who supply it. Advice is a form of nostalgia. Dispensing it is a way of fishing the past from the disposal, wiping it off, painting over the ugly parts and recycling it for more than it's worth.

But trust me on the sunscreen.

The secret to happiness is keeping your mind on the things you want and off the things you don't want.

Earl Nightingale

An ancient legend tells the story of a wise old hermit who lived in a log cabin high in the mountains. He was reputed to know the answer to any question ever brought to him.

One day, two mischievous boys decided they were going to play a trick on the old fellow. They would ask him a question he couldn't answer!

After plotting one night high in the loft of a dark barn, they shot a blinding light into a sparrow's eye. Quickly they picked the stunned bird up and made their way to the old man's cabin. One of them could feel the bird's frightened, fluttering heartbeat in his hand as he held it snugly.

Now, with their hands behind their back they would pull a trick on the old man. They'd say, "What do we have in our hands?" And if he guessed a bird, they'd say, "What kind of bird?" If he guessed the sparrow, then they would trap him. They would ask the trick question, "Tell us wise one, is it dead or alive?" If he said, "alive," they would squeeze the life out of the sparrow and prove him wrong. If he said, "dead," they'd prove him wrong again by simply letting the little creature fly.

They walked up the mountain trail, flashed the light on the log cabin and knocked on the door. They waited nervously, their shaky hands behind them. The heavy door squeaked slowly open. There stood a huge old man with long hair and a white beard hanging almost to his waist. He glowered at them through his narrow eyes and said, "What is it my boys?"

Excited, they answered, "Sir, wise old man, tell us if you can, what do we hold in our hands?" His eyes pierced through them. He waited. Then he spoke, "A bird." They said, "Well, sir, what kind of bird?" "A sparrow." They poked each other. "Tell us old man, is it dead or alive?"

He looked and looked and thought and finally he spoke, "As you will have it my boys. It is in your hands." Likewise, it's your life—it's in your hands...you decide.

YOU CAN HAVE AN INCREDIBLE LIFE!